Faith, Doubt, Mystery

Praise for Faith, Doubt, Mystery

James Tracy's *Faith, Doubt, Mystery* features challenges of faith and challenges of the heart. In the end, this amazing tale is intelligently told and finds redemption in unusual and rewarding places.

Charles R. Cross, Author, *Heavier than Heaven*

In *Faith, Doubt, Mystery*, James Tracy has written a well-tempered memoir, one that will ring true to anyone who has undergone a crisis of faith. In retracing the steps of his journey as a Jesuit seminarian, he manages to evoke that peculiar affection that we feel toward our own younger, more idealistic selves. Tracy's trek is a small victory for us all.

Gary Miranda, Author, *Listeners at the Breathing Place, Grace Period*

James Tracy's *Faith, Doubt and Mystery* is a beautifully written exploration of meaning and mystery. His growing insights are deep and life-affirming, his writing is powerful and elegant, his metaphors are brilliant. His memoir is filled with courage, wisdom, and hope. For anyone ready to examine the mystery of life's meaning it is a must read.

Carlene Cross, Author, *The Undying West, Fleeing Fundamentalism*

Faith, Doubt, Mystery

A CATHOLIC JOURNEY

James J. Tracy

ISBN: 1514857537
ISBN 13: 9781514857533

Dedication

For My Family—Past, Present, and Future

Altar boy: *"I will go to the altar of God, to God, the joy of my youth."*

Priest: *"I will still praise Thee on the harp, O God, my God. Why are you sad, O my soul, and why do you trouble me?"*

--From prayers at the beginning of the Mass

Contents

Prologue

"Grandpa, were you a priest?" my granddaughter asked.

"No, I was a seminarian for a long time and almost a priest."

"Oh."

And with that single syllable the thirteen-year-old turned back to the sink where she finished scrubbing the dinner pots and pans.

I thought she might pursue my answer with another question since we were the only ones in the kitchen, but then I remembered she'd not been raised Catholic. "Priest" and "seminarian" likely drifted with "martyr" and "pope" on a sea of vague recognition. Now, my guess is she felt uncomfortable pushing into unfamiliar waters.

My granddaughter's question took me back to a still-vivid memory during Holy Week, in the early days of April 1966. Several other Jesuit seminarians and I had come down from our theological college in the foothills of the Santa Cruz Mountains to a large church in the Santa Clara Valley. We came garbed in our cassocks and Roman collars, indistinguishable from ordained priests, to assist in the Easter liturgy for the large Catholic community that ranged from executives, who lived well in the surrounding hills, to Hispanic laborers, who worked hard in the vineyards that lined the hillsides.

The warm breeze through the open window of the Volkswagen van soothed the heat that kept rising as we chugged closer to the parking area next to the church. As I stepped out of the van, my foot stirred the dust. A gust of wind came up. It briefly ballooned my cassock into a black parachute.

Our parking spot bordered the path, where I heard the rapid exchange of Spanish among a group of young men making their way toward the church entrance. Seeing us, one young man broke away from his companions and ran up to me. He fell on his knees at my feet and looked up with hands pressed together in prayerful entreaty. Surprise and lack of Spanish slowed my understanding that he wanted a priestly blessing. My companions were a few steps ahead of me and didn't notice my predicament as they continued to make their way toward the church. As I looked down at this young Catholic with his glistening black hair and caramel complexion, I felt his faith as palpably as the bright sun and warm air.

I thought, *I don't speak Spanish, and even if I did, I can't quickly explain the difference between a seminarian and a priest. Besides, even if I could make that point, it doesn't meet his need. He wants my blessing, pure and simple*

And with that I raised both my hands, arcing them slowly upward until my fingers met at eye level. My right hand broke free to trace a cross as I softly said, "It will do you no good, it will do you no harm, in the name of the Father, and of the Son, and of the Holy Spirit." Then I pressed my hands firmly on his bent head. He looked up smiling and closed our brief encounter with, "Muchas gracias, Padre."

It took me a few minutes to catch up with my companions, but much longer to untangle the knotted skein of thoughts within me: *This was no joke. It was the best honest blessing I could give a young man who has no doubts about his faith. I'm an imposter.*

After almost ten years in the Jesuit Order, I was closing in on ordination as a Catholic priest. I thought of the seed my parents had planted, Catholic schools had nurtured, and the Society of Jesus had enriched. Up to this point I had moved forward assisted solely by the elementary-school theology of the Baltimore Catechism. Only in the last year-and-a half had I begun the formal study of theology. Now, in the swirl of courses on the Nature & Mission of the Church, Moral Theology, Revelation, Biblical Inspiration, the Act of Faith, and Canon Law, I was plagued with doubts, doubts about the doctrines that slept beneath the dream of my becoming a priest, a dream I had pursued for over twenty years. Questions cycloned inside me: *What was I doing? Where was I going? How had I gotten here?*

CHAPTER 1
The Beginning

GOOD NEWS

I was six-years-old. I knew March 1944 was the best month of my life, because I had received first Holy Communion on the first Sunday of the month. I kept thinking about how I'd closed my eyes and opened my mouth wide enough to receive the white host. I made sure not to chew. "Let it soften until you can swallow it," Sister Francella had said. I knew from the Catechism I had received the body of Christ.

And today brought good news and another first. I was subbing for my eleven-year-old brother, Ron. I would be in charge of his *Seattle Times* paper stand, just south of the Sears & Roebuck's store at 65th and Roosevelt Way. My excitement pushed me to walk faster along the ten blocks between home and the stand. On the way, I gave the Hollywood Theatre a quick glance. On most Saturdays I'd see a double feature with Gene Autry or Roy Rogers catching cattle rustlers and, in between, newsreels of the war against the Nazis and the Japanese. But I didn't mind missing the movies, because I'd be selling newspapers.

The paper stand stood wedged between Rhodes Dime Store and Bartell Drugs. Layers of dark-green paint covered its pitted and splintered shelves. Its sides stood five-feet high with a middle shelf that could hold two stacks of papers. There I took my post.

Ron, the night before, had coached me. "Mr. Mahoney drives pretty fast when he's dropping off papers. Don't stand too close to the curb, because the kid who pushes the bundles out from the back seat opens the door before the car stops. You don't want to get hit with the open door. And Mr. Mahoney would be mad if you got hit. Do you understand?"

I had nodded "Yes," looking directly into Ron's agate-blue eyes. I always looked up to my brother because he was older and knew a lot more than me. I learned to sell papers from watching him at the stand—how to drag the two Saturday bundles back to the stand, cut the twine with his pocket knife, and quickly pile the papers on the shelf because regular customers were waiting.

I'm sure Ron had talked to Mom about my filling in for him. Mom had a quiet way of orchestrating decisions and controlling what followed. She knew I'd tagged along enough with Ron to know how to sell the papers, how to hold the paper against my chest so the headlines showed, and how to sort the coins into the money apron. I didn't like asking people, who were walking fast and looking straight ahead, "Paper, Sir? Paper, Ma'am?" I could tell before they got to me that they had other things on their minds and were heading someplace important. But I kept in mind what Ron had said. "I have to pay for all the papers that are dropped off, not just for the ones we sell. You need to sell every one of them or come real close."

An older gentleman, stately and tall in his long, charcoal overcoat, often stood waiting for the bus next to the stand. The Bartell awning protected both of us from the chilly wind gusting along the sidewalk. I always stood on the opposite side of Ron when the two of them talked. Ron said the man had explained stocks to him because that's how he made his money. But today he was next to me.

As we huddled under the awning, he told me Franklin Roosevelt wasn't such a good president, because he did things that weren't good for the country. I knew from Mom and Dad that President Roosevelt saved the country during the Depression. Roosevelt, in my Catholic first-grader mind, stood in the top row of people in the world, right next to Pope Pius XII. But I kept my thoughts to myself and didn't look sideways, which wasn't hard because we stood facing the traffic like two manikins. I noticed goulashes on men's feet and umbrellas women struggled to control. Most of all, I stood alert for cars pulling close to the curb with the window down and a hand with exact change waiting for the paper. As I listened to the gentleman's criticism of Roosevelt, my vision blurred. I looked at the passing cars as if they were going into fog. The people faded away, and purple arrived. I felt my head turn toward my elderly companion and I heard myself say, "I think I'm going to be sick."

I woke up in Bartell's bright back room looking up at the lady from Van de Kamp's Bakery in her white uniform topped off with a Dutch girl's cap. She was telling the manager she'd called my mother.

BAD NEWS

Dr. Gregg came to the house with his black bag, which held a cold stethoscope that made me shiver when he put it on my bare chest. I overheard him say to Mom and Dad, "It will be about two weeks before we know whether it's polio or rheumatic fever, because the symptoms are the same."

I soaked up what the doctor had said, together with the brief exchanges between my folks. I learned then how unaware parents can be; little pitchers do have big ears. I felt the heat of fever, the tiredness that made it hard to roll over, and the aches in my shoulders and knees. As I dozed off, I thought polio would be better than rheumatic fever, because I might get my picture on a poster with crutches and my legs in braces like President Roosevelt.

Ron (10) and Jimmie (5)

I slept a lot over the next ten days, mostly on the davenport in the living room across from our Sylvania radio, which was almost as big as a jukebox. Mom let me keep it on low all the time. It became my companion with the comedy of Jack Benny and the mystery of *The Shadow* with Lamont Cranston.

On Wednesday Dr. Gregg called before noon to talk to Mom and ask whether my legs had become floppy. I remember her telling Dad, when he came home, that the doctor had decided I had rheumatic fever, not polio. He'd said my heart had been infected and was overworking, inflating like a balloon to the point where it pushed against my rib cage. I was sure if it popped, I would die. I wasn't afraid, because I had gone to Confession, not committed any big sins, and had received Jesus in Holy Communion.

The next day around five o'clock, while dozing and listening to the radio, I heard, "We interrupt this program to announce that today, April 12, 1945, this afternoon at 3:35 Eastern time, President Roosevelt died." I called out to Mom in the kitchen. She came in just as the announcer was repeating his message. I felt tears running down my cheeks. Mom wrapped her arms around me. That's the first time I cried about a person I'd never talked to. I wondered whether President Roosevelt knew he was dying when it was happening.

What is it like to die? I wondered again whether I would die from rheumatic fever. I knew I would die someday. The Catechism said when in danger of death, we should receive the sacrament of Extreme Unction, in which a priest would anoint us with oil and say prayers to give our souls strength. The Catechism held a lot of Church teachings. I didn't understand all of them, but I was good at memorizing and repeating answers back word for word.

CHANGES

My hope of becoming a poster child for polio faded away. My folks gave me their bedroom on the first floor while they moved up the narrow stairs to the second floor with its low sloping ceilings where Ron and I had a bedroom. The switch of bedrooms took away the exertion of climbing stairs. Bed rest included not getting up to go the bathroom. I had to wait for Mom to slip the metal pan under me.

Rheumatic fever got me out of school. I didn't have to go back to first grade, which was not all bad because I was sometimes scared of Sister Francella, whose brown Italian eyes turned storm-dark when my words froze up in reading group. When I learned she had passed me into second grade, I felt the tightness in my body ease. I guess she was nicer than I thought.

About this time Grandma Bury, Mom's mom, moved from Minneapolis to live with us. There was no reason for Grandma to stay in cold Minnesota after Grandpa died, so Mom, being the oldest child, took her in. Grandma Bury was shorter than Mom, maybe five-feet tall. She was much heavier, but not real fat. She wore glasses that stayed on by pinching her nose—*pince-nez* spectacles Mom told me, just like President Roosevelt's.

I'd never met Grandma before, but she fit right in like she'd always been part of our family. She didn't give a lot of hugs but when she did, they were warm and firm. She didn't fuss over my being sick and certainly didn't give any pity. I knew Mom liked her joining our family full-time. Sometimes the two of them sat at the kitchen table eating pickled pigs' feet for lunch and talking for more than an hour. When they didn't want me to know what they were talking about, they'd speak German. That's when I learned that Mom spoke only German until she started grade school in Long Prairie, Minnesota. Lots of German immigrants had moved to Minnesota in the early 1900s.

By June, I was up and using the bathroom and going up the stairs to the bedroom with Ron. Mom and Dad got their bedroom back. In the summer my folks moved us less than a mile north to a bigger house on 91st Street where there was a level six-block walk to St. Catherine's School. The house came with a bedroom for Grandma that was as big as Mom and Dad's. Ron and I got an upstairs bedroom with walls and a sloped ceiling all covered in varnished knotty pine.

By September, I was ready for second grade and my new teacher Sister Rebecca. She was a big woman—taller than Mom, who was five-feet-two, but not as tall as Dad, who was six-feet-two. Sister Rebecca's garniture, the nun's head gear circling her head and looking like a calla lily, framed a freckled face younger than Mom's. She smiled a lot, and didn't frown when we gave a wrong answer. I wasn't scared, as I had been in the first grade, and was able to answer without freezing up. Asking questions was still hard, so I took them home and asked Mom.

THE QUARANTINE

Mom and I were the first ones up and in the kitchen one Saturday morning. She was wearing her bathrobe covered with a print of red and yellow flowers. I was still in my pajamas. She stood in front of the stove waiting for the coffee to start percolating. I'd taken the Wheaties and milk to the kitchen table.

After sitting down, I said, "Mom, Sister Rebecca said it was a sin to play by myself."

"What?" she said as she turned and looked at me.

"When I'm in the bedroom playing by myself with my cars, I don't see why that's a sin."

"I don't think Sister Rebecca was talking about playing *by* yourself," she said.

"That's what she said."

"I think she meant something else."

"Then what did she mean?"

Mom stood frozen, staring at a spot high on the wall above my head. After several seconds, she placed both hands on the front of her bathrobe below her waist and rapidly rubbed them up and down a couple of times. Then she turned and left the kitchen.

I sat puzzled with my Wheaties. After sifting through what she said along with her strange hand motions, I concluded it was OK for me to play alone with my toys in the bedroom. Mom didn't come back, so I had to turn down the heat under the throbbing coffee pot. That began and ended my parent-delivered sex education. Dad never went there.

That incident awakened an awareness of a space inside me where I put thoughts and reactions I didn't think proper to say out loud. Some were questions I just knew should be quarantined, like kids with chickenpox; some were observations that puzzled me or didn't fit with what I already knew; some were too scary to address at the moment and needed to be put away for later. That's where I put Mom's hand motions that Saturday morning. I came to regard that space inside as my "quarantine."

ROUND TWO

My biggest problem in school was not the homework, but the rule Dr. Gregg had imposed: "No running and no games requiring even moderate physical exertion." Mom had passed the edict on to the Sisters of Providence, especially Sister Rebecca. *But how could I not run at recess or in the neighborhood with my friends Ricky and David?*

By the spring, I got good at working my way to the far side of the playground, where I began to play tag and break into short runs. Only a few times did Sister Rebecca catch me running at recess. When she did, her scolding was soft, as if she really didn't like doing it.

Every other week, Sister herded all of us second-graders across the skinny patch of asphalt to the church for Confession. Sometimes I had to dream up sins to confess—because not having a sin to confess was a sure sign of saying you're perfect, and that certainly was a sin. But somehow it didn't cross my mind that running at recess was a sin of disobeying my parents. And it never occurred to me that inventing sins to confess was a lie. I hadn't yet developed a grammar good enough to parse all the sins.

After school was out for the summer, I increased the running and playing by slipping away after lunch to join Ricky and David for three-man baseball games. This routine got easy after Mom started working, because Grandma usually napped in the early afternoon. Besides, from the house she couldn't see where we were playing.

I felt alive and strong most of the time in June. Then the aches began to come back, my breath ran short when I was chasing down the ball, and I began to have nosebleeds again. Just before the fried-chicken Sunday dinner to celebrate my mid-July birthday, I fainted. I woke up in Mom and Dad's bed hearing Dad scolding Ron for not watching me and saying half-angry, half-worried, "He's down again."

I heard what Dad said, and I knew Ron wasn't to blame for my running. But Ron didn't defend himself. He even stepped back from his first-born advantage and yielded to me most of our parents' attention while I was sick.

The setback filled my head with the image of a ballooned heart. *Had I been playing tag with death?* Rheumatic fever was leaving a more indelible mark. It stamped me with an awareness of life's limit, not death's imminence. The mixture of fever and faith made me keenly alert to what comes after life—heaven or hell. Purgatory didn't count much, because it was just a stopover to purify us on the road to heaven. At times I thought, *When I'm 15, Ron will be 20; when I'm 30, he'll be 35.* For some reason I never got to 50. Whether I didn't think I would live that long or just was unable to imagine Ron being 55, I never figured out. I would stare at the picture of Grandma Tracy on the bureau opposite the bed. She died two years before I was born. I wished I'd known what she was like. But I knew what rheumatic fever was like and what it meant: Stay in bed, sleep a lot, and wait for the muscle aches to pass.

SEARCHING

When Mom started working, Grandma looked after me. She would come in to spend time with me and listen to "Queen for a Day" on the plastic Emerson radio that sat on the bed stand. To avoid hearing the squeal of ladies who'd won a year's supply of Duz soap, "the soap that does everything," I learned to fake sleep. My closed eyes triggered Grandma to turn off the radio and shut the bedroom door behind her.

After the first days of tiredness lifted, boredom settled in. I searched for a way to get closer to God. I found it next to the radio—my parents' Bible. I resolved to read it cover to cover. But when the Genesis genealogy got rolling, "The descendants of Japheth are Gomer, Magog, Madi, Javan, Thubal, Mosoch and Thiras," my resolution softened like butter left out on the kitchen table.

I still wanted to do something God would like. I asked Ron to bring me his *Baltimore Catechism.* It turned out to be *Baltimore Catechism, No. 2,* the one for the upper grades. It had all the same questions and answers as the lower grades *No. 1,* plus a lot more. Reading the questions jump-started the answers I'd memorized in second grade. I began to review and memorize answers.

6. Q. Why did God make you?
A. God made me to know Him, to love Him, and to serve Him in this world, and to be happy with Him forever in the next.
13. Q. What is God?
A. God is a spirit infinitely perfect.
14. Q. Had God a beginning?
A. God had no beginning; He always was and He always will be.

I remembered asking Sister Rebecca the previous spring, "Who made up the questions and answers." She said bishops had met in Baltimore in the 1880s and made them up. I wanted to ask whether the pope had checked their work because I'd been told that he was infallible and couldn't make a mistake. Later I learned he could make a mistake in arithmetic, but not when it came to "faith and morals."

As summer crept to an end, I began spending time alone during the day in the backyard. Lying on the coarse Army-surplus blanket spread out on the grass, I found the warm August days demanded nothing of my muscles. The leafy cover of the cherry tree kept me safe from direct sunlight.

My thoughts drifted back to the preparation for First Communion before rheumatic fever first put me in bed and before President Roosevelt had died. I had learned that only a priest, who had the power to change bread and wine into the body and blood of Christ, could give Communion. A priest also had the power to forgive sins. I knew there couldn't be better work than that of a priest helping people get to heaven to spend eternity with God.

I gazed upward toward the sunlight flickering through the leaves above me and began to review again who God was and why He made me. *Forever, infinitely, no beginning,* and *always* floated through my mind and wrapped me in a feeling as good as a hug. Looking toward the blue sky over house next door, I squinted and raced my mind to chase the "forever" of God, repeating the word in gong rhythms inside my head, *Forever and forever and forever* until pleasant dizziness pressed me deeper into the cushion of the blanket on the grass. Maybe that's why I repeated the dizzying ritual in the backyard in the last days of summer. It felt good.

SURPRISES

As the start of third grade drew closer, Dr. Gregg encouraged my parents to extend my home rest and delay my return to school. They decided to wait until late September. Two surprises cushioned my disappointment over not returning to St. Catherine's for the start of third grade.

I had just awakened from a late afternoon nap on our stiff davenport, feeling cozy under the warm wool reds of the afghan Grandma had knitted just before I was born. I had always believed the afghan helped me go to sleep faster and deeper, as it had that afternoon. I remember thinking it was odd that Mom and Grandma were both sitting in the living room when I woke up. I thought they might be worrying I would throw up on the afghan, like I did just after the fever had come back.

A knock at the front door hurried Mom to open it. I looked up to see Father Doogan, the assistant pastor, who the church ladies thought was handsome. A priest had never been to our house before. I didn't think I was sick enough for him to give me Extreme Unction. He smiled and sat on the dining room chair Mom brought for him. He asked whether I wanted to receive Holy Communion. I said, "Yes." He stood up and stepped toward me as he unbuttoned his suit coat. I saw the pyx hanging on a cord around his neck. It was gold and about the size of Dad's railroad watch. I knew it held consecrated Communion wafers. He opened it carefully and took out a single host. He traced a cross with the host and placed it on my tongue. No one talked until I opened my eyes after thanking God for visiting me and after I'd swallowed the host.

Father then began telling me how God always looked after me as He did for all His creatures. He went on to say that God loved me, and how He wanted me to love Him in return. He said God always did things for a reason; even my rheumatic fever had a reason in God's mind. He said God's gift of illness to people often means they're special.

Mom and Dad circa 1946

As Father Doogan was talking, Dad came in from work carrying a large brown paper bag, the kind with twine handles strong enough to hold lots of groceries. Father Doogan's words ran out as Dad went to Mom and held the bag down so she could peek in, but not low enough for me to see. He did the same for Grandma and Father Doogan. No one said anything. Then without letting me see inside the bag, he walked over and spilled what was in it on the afghan. A black cocker spaniel puppy squirmed on my lap until my petting settled him down and he found just the right spot to curl up next to me.

That day ended with my feeling the warmth of the Church, my family, and my first dog, Toby.

CHAPTER 2

Recovery

L ate September and the start of third grade didn't come fast enough for me. Mom and I walked the six straight level blocks from our house to St. Catherine's School. Mom was wearing her best gray suit, probably because she would be talking to the principal and my new teacher, Sister Paula. Mom usually walked pretty fast, but this day she let me set the pace. Several times she gave me a sideways glance, probably checking to see if I was getting winded or whether there was a glisten of sweat on my forehead. I knew she was taking no chances on my having a third-round of rheumatic fever.

Going into the third grade, I didn't feel afraid as I had as a first-grader. But I didn't know what kind of teacher Sister Paula would be, how she would treat me, and how far behind I was in class. I knew I wouldn't know everyone in class, because new families often moved into the parish during summer vacation.

Mom and I went through the front door and up the few steps to the first-floor office, where Sister Agnes stood waiting for us. I could see gray hairs in her eyebrows and a couple of whiskers on her chin just like Grandma had. She said Sister Paula would be expecting me. The second class period had already begun. That left the hall and stairways eerily quiet. The three of us climbed the polished steps to the second floor.

Sister Agnes tapped her ring on the glass window in the door of classroom number eight. Sister Paula came out into the hallway. I was surprised at how young she looked. Her face, snugged into the Providence nun's garniture, looked like the beautiful teenage sister of my friend Gary. She smiled at Mom and Sister Agnes, took my hand and, without a word, led me into class. Holding my hand, she said, "Jimmie Tracy is back in school with us." I liked her saying "us." I got big smiles from the kids who knew me from first and second grades. I found my desk at the back of the class with the others whose last names came at the end of the alphabet. In settling in and looking at what had been put inside my desk, I had forgotten to look at the door to see if Mom was watching. When I did, she was gone.

Over those first weeks of catching up on class work, I couldn't help looking at Sister Paula when she wasn't looking my way. Her skin was as milky white as the marble of the Virgin Mary statue in the church next door; it certainly wasn't as dark as Sister Francella's, who had scared me two years before. And she was not as tall and thick as second-grade Sister Rebecca. Sister Paula's voice was light and clear, almost like a flute, when she read stories to the class after lunch.

In religion class a few weeks later, after she had called on three classmates to recite the answers they'd memorized for the Catechism questions, she added, "Jesus has taught us it's important to love everyone."

The itch of a question raised my hand. "Everyone?" I asked.

"Yes, everyone."

"Even the Japs?" I added.

"Yes, even the Japanese," she corrected.

Well-schooled by bloody war-in-the-Pacific news reels that had come in the middle of the Saturday double feature at the Hollywood Theater, I added "So we're supposed to love people who were killing Americans last year?"

"Yes, the Japanese are people who suffered like Americans, and Jesus loves them too."

After dinner that night I complained to Mom about what Sister Paula had said.

"Sister's right," Mom said. "The Japanese are people too, and it's important to try to love everybody."

Just over a year ago we were killing these enemies by the thousands at Iwo Jima and Okinawa and they were killing thousands of Americans too. Now, we're supposed to love them? It didn't make sense, but I didn't say anything.

A Visitor

Not long after that, Mom said a visitor was coming from Portland for Sunday dinner. She added that he was the son of a man Dad had worked with on the railroad, a man who'd been kind to Dad and her when they were first married. Dad's friend, Ray Ishii, worked as a mechanic repairing engines and passenger cars in a railroad shop close by. He finagled to get Dad a handcar to take Mom up the line to see sights along the Columbia River. She smiled as she described Dad pumping the little car's handles up and down like a teeter-totter as they shot along on the tracks.

Mom went on to say that after Ron was born, she and Dad invited Ray and his family to come to Portland for Sunday dinner. That's when she met Ray, Jr., who was a teenager when I was born. Mom said he was coming for Sunday dinner just as he used to come with his parents before the war. I didn't think much about it until Sunday, when I saw Mom rolling drumsticks in flour. Fried chicken was a special dinner and one of my favorites.

When I came in to wash up for dinner, Ray was sitting talking to my folks. He was wearing a dark suit with a striped tie.

His black shoes shined like mirrors. I always noticed men's shoes because Dad said the care a man gives his shoes can tell you a lot about the man. Ray's hair was the color of his shoes and slicked smooth with tonic that made it shine. Dad said, "Jimmie, I'd like you to meet Ray Ishii, the son of a very good friend of mine."

I don't remember putting out my hand, but do remember how his hand was warmer than mine. When Ray was looking away from me at Dad or Ron, I'd study his face, the way he moved his hands, and how his voice and perfect English didn't sound like the sly voices of the Japanese officers portrayed in war movies.

Later, after dinner when Ray was gone, Mom told me that he and his whole family had been "interned" (another name for being put in prison) during the war. Even though they were all American citizens and Ray's father had worked a long time on the railroad with a lot of other Japanese, they were all sent away to a camp in Idaho with barbwire and guards.

My patriotic prejudice had been well-fed by the propaganda of the day. World War II newspapers frequently displayed caricatures and cartoons of Japanese leaders like Emperor Hirohito and Prime Minister Tojo. Second-run movies highlighted the mistreatment of heroic Americans. The internment of Japanese Americans was never mentioned.

That night, before I went to bed, the faces of Ray Ishii, Sister Paula, and Mom and Dad swirled inside me. As I knelt next to my bed to say my evening prayers, I caught a glimmer of my mistake. I promised God I'd never again use the word "Japs."

MOM

Scrolling through memories of Mom, I find them brimming with strength, a resource I turned to, especially when I was scared.

"They're going to beat me up," I whined.

It was early in the first grade, before I got sick and while we still lived on Roosevelt Way. The day before, half a block from home, three older boys, who must have been 10 or 11, stopped me and asked where I was going. After I said, "St. Catherine's," they started saying things about "Catholics" and stood real close to me. I was scared and had to walk on a lawn to get around them. They didn't punch me, but I thought they were going to. They yelled something at me, but I was going as fast as I could without running.

It was the next morning that I spilled out my fright to Mom.

"I just know they're going to beat me up," I repeated.

"No, they won't," Mom said.

But those words didn't chase away my jitters.

"Will you walk me past the corner at the end of the block?"

Mom was still in her bathrobe and wasn't going to walk me to school or past the scary corner dressed like that.

After listening to more worry and whining, she said, "I'll stand out on the sidewalk where you can see me and I can see you all the way past that corner."

Knowing this was what I'd have to settle for, off I went no less scared, but knowing Mom would do something when those boys started beating me up. As I drew closer to the corner I turned my head to see if Mom was still on the sidewalk watching me. She was. As I crossed from 75th to 76th I glanced to my right to see how close the bullies were. No one was in sight. I increased my steps, but not before I turned and waved at Mom. She waved back. I was safe.

Bits and pieces of Mom and Dad's life before Ron and I were born leaked out. I always wanted to know what it was like for them growing up, but I'd learned asking too many questions wasn't welcome. Listening and piecing together guesses worked pretty well.

Although Mom was not tall, she commanded respect. I think that began with her standing as the oldest of four children, and the only girl. She was an only child until she was five. Grandma told me that not long after the birth of her first son, Mom went into her baby brother's room to see him. A shrill infant cry hurried Grandma into find Mom next to the crib. In picking up baby Ray, Grandma noticed a bite mark on his hand. In answering why she had bitten her brother, Mom had answered, "Because I love him so much."

I'm sure that confidence grew stronger in her early twenties before she met Dad. At the time, she was working for a Minneapolis lawyer during prohibition. Her boss defended men connected with Al Capone. With a smile she described going with her boss to a mansion where there was drinking and gambling. A man in a tuxedo guided her around while her boss met with bigwigs. She told the man watching over her that she wanted to try gambling. When he offered her money to play, she said she'd brought her own. He smiled and said, "Use ours, because you can't win." She accepted his offer.

Mom's strength could be pleasant and persistent. That's probably why our pastor, Father Beglin, recognized her as a good fit for working on the annual St. Catherine's bazaar. He figured out that she'd be good at sweet-talking store owners out of expensive items that became prizes at the bazaar. The day before the bazaar began Mom took me after school to the lunchroom, where she was organizing all the prizes. Father Beglin came in to talk about final preparations. I saw this towering, beefy priest looking down at Mom and paying close attention to what she was saying. They seemed strangely equal.

I also knew Father Beglin as the priest who always stepped into every classroom at the start of each school year. His size and booming voice made me think of a papa bear checking on his cubs. At other times, when he was serious or angry about someone misbehaving, I always slid lower in my seat even though I knew he wasn't mad at me.

Dad

Grandma Tracy raised Dad Catholic. His father was a railroad engineer who was away a lot and drank a lot. Once I heard Dad tell a neighbor who was offering him a second drink, "No thanks, my father did enough drinking for the both of us." I figured out Dad worked hard from old photos and the few stories he told about growing up, like at age twelve currying and grooming horses before school. I pieced together that was how he earned money to help his mom make ends meet. At sixteen, Mom said, he was working at a butcher shop when a meat grinder caught his right hand and took off four fingers down to the first joint.

I did like watching the face of a man meeting Dad and shaking hands for the first time. I'd see that surprised look followed by a quick glance down at their clasped hands. I never heard anyone ask him a question about his missing fingers. Mom told me Dad did get really irritated once with a guy who started asking lots of questions about how he lost his fingers. She said Dad didn't answer him at first. Finally, he told him he fell off a boat in the Mississippi River and got run over by a paddle-wheeler.

Best of all, I liked to watch Dad write. His thumb would hold his Waterman's pen against the stump of his first finger. Then the neatest writing would flow out of the gleaming silver tip. I wondered whether Dad believed it was God's will that he should lose his fingers like I was told it was God's will that I got rheumatic fever. I never found the right time to ask him.

Dad wasn't able to volunteer at church as much as Mom because he worked a lot of overtime. I did know he was a good Catholic because on some Sundays, when the assistant pastor was hearing confessions at the back of the church, he'd go to the telephone-booth-size confessional. I guessed that's when he'd get forgiven for his "goddam son-of-a-bitch" that broke out sometimes when he hit himself while hammering or having a hard time getting a wrench to fit in a tight place.

As a family we usually went to the ten o'clock Sunday Mass because Dad often worked overtime on Saturday and Mom let him sleep in. That Mass was the one Father Beglin would celebrate. The pastor's voice reached every corner of the church without any sound system, which came years later. His sermons usually ended with a strong request to be generous in giving to the Church.

During my first Sunday Mass back, after my second bout of rheumatic fever, we drove to church as we always did—Dad wearing a suit and tie, Mom in a Sunday dress, coat, and hat. Ron and I usually came in white shirts and salt-and-pepper cords. Grandma Bury wore her long black coat covering her best dress and, like Mom, a hat to cover her hair because St. Paul said something about hair being a woman's "glory." I really didn't get that.

I soon felt the stuffiness of the crowded church. By the offertory of the Mass I was light-headed. A queasy stomach arrived by the consecration. I turned to Dad beside me and said, "I think I might be getting sick."

"Can you make it out the door by yourself?" he asked.

"I think so."

I slipped out of the pew and tip-toed toward the rear doors. It was just my luck to be leaving right before Communion. When Father Beglin turned toward the congregation with the raised host, he caught sight of me nearing the rear exit.

"Somebody stop that boy!" he shouted.

I froze, felt tears coming up; I didn't know what to do.

Dad stood up in his pew in the middle of the kneeling congregation and yelled back, "He's sick."

He left his pew and led me out to the car. Dad was quiet. He rolled down the window to let in fresh air. When Mass was over and the rest of the family was back in the car, I didn't have to get into the back seat with Grandma and Ron. I rode home in the front seat between Dad and Mom. What stuck in my mind was Dad's publicly shouting back at a priest. I'd never seen or heard anyone disagree with a priest publicly like Dad had done.

The shock of Dad's actions fit with what I heard the month before. When I came in for lunch, Mom and Grandma were talking about the picture on the front page of the *Northwest Progress*, the Diocese of Seattle's paper sent to all parishioners. In a front-page photo Bishop Connelly, in his Mass vestments, was holding his bishop's crozier, the metal staff symbolizing a bishop as a shepherd leading his flock. Grouped around him was a Catholic family with the mother holding her twelfth child. I knew parents who reached a dozen kids always got their picture on the front page.

"I don't think poor planning deserves a front-page picture," Mom said. "I don't agree with having that many kids."

Grandma said, "I remember a lady in Long Prairie who went to the priest complaining that she couldn't have more children because she and her husband couldn't afford to feed them. Do you know what he said?"

Mom stayed silent.

Grandma went on, "He didn't say anything. He just gave her a rosary. I would have thrown it back at him."

Both Mom and Grandma at the same time noticed my open-mouth stare. Grandma lowered her voice and switched into German.

I'd never heard anyone in our family criticize a priest or get angry with something the Church thought was a good idea. I quarantined what I'd heard.

MY CATHOLIC FAMILY

My folks were not Catholics as strict as some of my friends' parents who made them kneel in their living room every night and say the rosary. We did say the rosary together at night a few times during Lent, but that was the extent of it. Still, I knew Mom and Dad were good Catholics.

Knowing my catechism was important, just like observing the Church law regarding no eating meat on Friday. I welcomed both practices as part of being a good Catholic and on a par with going to church on Sunday. I liked best the Fridays when we all rode down to the *Spud* on Green Lake Way. The *Spud* had the best fish and chips in town. Almost everyone bought take-out because there was no room to sit inside, even too crowded to wait there for your order. The owners had wired up a loudspeaker outside so people could sit in their cars until their number was called. Fridays brought the longest wait, because Catholics flocked to the *Spud* like hungry seagulls.

In the fall and winter, tightly closed car windows and a full-blast heater filled the car with the smell of fish and chips. My hunger teamed up with the smell to make the ride home seem just short of forever. At home, Dad would break the pieces of fish as carefully as Father Beglin broke the big host at Mass. Each of us got at least half a piece of fish, about the size of a playing card. I'd dip my fish into the small paper cup filled with tartar sauce and follow it up with a French fry dipped in ketchup. Those fish and chips tasted better than the best forbidden-on-Friday hamburger.

It felt good being Catholic, a feeling warm and right, but sometimes too tight.

CHAPTER 3

Grade School Faith

THE SACRIFICES OF LENT

I'd never seen any of my Protestant friends have anything as special as the mark of Ash Wednesday, the black smudge on the forehead. Even after school when I went home and played with my non-Catholic friends, I never brushed off a single cinder.

Ash Wednesday started the clock on the forty days leading up to Easter. It marked a day when even Dad would come to church midweek if he was working nights. Before the first period, every student in school marched into church where we'd eagerly wait in our pews until signaled to kneel at the Communion rail like we did when receiving Holy Communion. Father Beglin would move back and forth along the rail with a dish filled with the ashes of burnt palm leaves. He'd first press his thumb into the dish and then imprint each of our foreheads. When we came out of church, some sported dark sooty marks while others left with faded ones that wore off quickly. I think the faded ones came from Father trying to stretch a single thumb-dip for three foreheads. I never washed off the ash because I'd come to see it as a special "Catholic" mark, a source of pride.

Lent was supposed to include giving things up and to run parallel to Jesus' life of sacrifice that ended with his crucifixion.

Tall, thin Sister Perpetua, my fourth-grade teacher, had schooled us in giving up things we liked. Not eating candy for forty days was a routine sacrifice for Catholic kids: no Baby Ruths, no Milk Duds, no Hershey Bars.

My sweet tooth also introduced me to the art of splitting hairs. Classmate Nancy asked Sister Perpetua whether saving candy until Lent was over and then eating it qualified as a real sacrifice. Because hoarding was what I did and what most of my friends did, the idea of giving up the post-Easter candy gorge seemed too big a sacrifice. I held my breath as sweet Sister Perpetua peered out the classroom window through her wire-rimmed glasses at the empty playground. I think she was searching for a Solomon answer to this tough question.

After an eternal ten seconds, she said, "Well, Nancy, that's a good question. I know Jesus values any and all sacrifices you make. I think he'll see giving up candy for all of Lent as one sacrifice and not eating it afterward as a second sacrifice. So it's up to each person to decide whether to make one or two sacrifices."

CHOSEN

The following September, when I was in the fifth grade and now ten years old, Father Beglin came to our classroom and handed me and three other boys neatly folded pieces of paper. Opening mine, I read a typed invitation to become an altar boy. Being one of four chosen a year early brought dizzying excitement. I was going to be on the altar in front of the congregation answering the priest in Latin, bringing him the wine to be consecrated, and holding the gold paten under the chins of those receiving Communion. I would be closer to God than I had ever been. I already had memorized the Latin responses to what the priest would say at Mass. And I knew what all the words meant. To the priest's opening *Introibo ad altare Dei* ("I will go to the altar of God"), I would answer, *Ad Deum, qui laetificat juventutem meam* ("To God who gives joy to my youth"). Experienced altar boys and the assistant pastor began teaching us the ritual's moves—when to ring the bells, when to genuflect, where to sit if the Mass had a sermon. Added to the splendor of serving Mass was the black cassock I could wear with a surplice, the white pullover tunic that covered the cassock from shoulder to waist. Best of all was the privilege and pride that came with serving God in this special way. When I started serving Mass, I often slipped into the reverie of one day being a priest who would be elevating the consecrated host, distributing Communion to extended tongues, and swinging the incense burner that billowed sweet clouds at high Mass. I'd let my priestly images run like Dad would let a big hooked salmon run until it was played out. Then I'd reel myself back as a fifth-grade altar boy.

SPEAKING UP

The sixth grade brought increasing strength. I now ran without getting winded quickly; I began speaking up in class; I sensed God was listening to my prayers. My confidence had starch.

I waited until after dinner when Dad was sitting in his favorite chair, dark green with padded arms that ended in wooden curlicues. There he would unwind by reading a book and smoking his pipe. The sweet smell of Sir Walter Raleigh tobacco hung in the living room. Mom was sitting across from him on the davenport knitting, a routine she developed since going to work in the yarn department of Frederick & Nelson.

"Dad, I want to get a paper route."

"Why would you like to do that?" he asked as he relaxed the book into his lap and took the pipe from his mouth.

"Well, I'd like to get a job to make some money so I can buy things I want."

"And what kind of things do you have in mind?

"A bicycle."

Ron had an Elgin bike the folks had bought for him at Sears & Roebuck's when we lived in Portland before the war. When I was four and five, Ron would let me sit on the seat with both arms wrapped around his waist while upright he'd pump uphill and coast downhill standing on the pedals. But now that bike, which was supposed to pass to me, was rusted with its front bearings worn out. I'd already stopped asking for a bike I knew my parents couldn't afford. My folks didn't talk about money in front of me or Ron or Grandma. I knew for sure money was tight, because Mom had taken her first job since getting married.

"And what paper route do you want to get?"

"I've already talked to Mike—he's a friend of David's who has a *Shopping News* route he's giving up. And it's only three days a week."

"It sounds like you have a plan." Dad looked over to Mom and said, "Ethel, what do you think?"

"How big a route is it?" Mom asked.

"It's 203 papers plus two extras."

"How much will you get paid?"

"It's seventy cents a delivery, over eight dollars a month."

Mom stretched the sleeve she'd been knitting and smoothed it out with her hand to check the evenness of the stitches before adding, "You know you'll have to deliver in all kinds of weather."

"Yes, I know."

"Are you sure you want to do it?"

"I really am. I told Mike I could start next week if it's alright with you and Dad. Mike said he'd take me on his delivery this

Thursday to show me all the streets and how to fold the papers for throwing."

"It's OK with me if it's OK with your father."

That brief exchange started me on a three-year run with *The Shopping News*. I had no idea where this urge came from. I only knew an inside part of me revved up when the chance came. My excitement triggered my offering Mike five dollars for his badly worn bag for toting the papers. The next week I found out I could have bought a new carrier bag from the newspaper for three dollars less. I regretted my failure to bargain, but not my getting the route.

I suspect Dad and Mom let me take the route because they were less worried about rheumatic fever returning, and they didn't want to squelch my idea. I think they'd done the same thing with Ron a few years before when he said he wanted to take up golf. He used money from selling papers to buy the clubs. Later he left the paper stand to caddy at a private golf course for money and the privilege of playing eighteen holes free once a week. Although Dad and Mom didn't understand golf or why Ron wanted to play, they didn't stop him from taking up the game.

THE PAPER ROUTE

In spite of increased strength, I soon came to realize my thin frame, which rheumatic fever had kept from exercise, couldn't carry all the papers at once. I had to figure out a way to get the job done. I decided to deliver the papers in two halves, coming back to the house to reload after I'd done the first half.

The Seattle rain soaked any papers that weren't covered with the delivery bag's canvas flap. Most often, the rain seeped through my pants below the knees and through the sleeves of my coat, while the bag kept my upper legs and body dry. During downpours, my socks squished. But I didn't mind, because on cold rainy days I'd soak in the bathtub after I got home and feel satisfied with working at my first job.

Rain was a quick-change artist—mist condensing to film on my coat sleeves, steady drizzles with soft rhythms, downpours that tap-tapped on the bill of my baseball cap, and wind-driven sheets that stung my face and narrowed my eyes to a squint. I wondered whether I could see as many different kinds of rain as my geography book said the Bedouins could see different shades of brown in the desert.

The rain and the papers became my companions as I plodded up and down the streets for three wet winters. No one seemed to notice me. But when I got home, Toby would bark and race down the stairs to the basement where I was hanging up the paper bag and my coat. I'd scoop him up, hold him tight, and talk to him before letting him go, a black furry blur scampering up the stairs to let Grandma know I was home.

QUESTIONS

The route gave me the privacy I came to look forward to, a time to think. Much as in the summertime spent recuperating in the backyard years five years before, my thoughts revolved around eternity and Catholic teachings. Sometimes I'd rehearse the answers in the Baltimore Catechism I'd memorized for religion class. Now I turned them over adding questions of my own.

ON THE UNITY AND TRINITY OF GOD

21. Q. Is there but one God?
A. Yes; there is but one God.

22. Q. Why can there be but one God?
A. There can be but one god, because God, being supreme and infinite, cannot have an equal.
23. Q. How many Persons are there in God?
A. In God there are three Divine Persons, really distinct, and equal in all things—the Father, the Son, and the Holy Ghost.

"Supreme" seems to be comparing God to something else. Supreme or highest of what? And there's "infinite" again. Numbers are infinite, because in arithmetic I know you can always add one to any number and repeat that addition forever. So what kind of infinite does God have? And three "really distinct" Persons in one God—what does that mean?

Questions had a life of their own. They just arrived unannounced. I quarantined many of them. Occasionally I wouldn't. In the seventh grade I read a story in the *Sacred Heart Messenger,* the monthly newsletter distributed to Catholic grade schools. The story praised a Catholic senator from Wisconsin, Joseph McCarthy. The article featured a picture of the senator eating breakfast at a small kitchen table just like people in the Kellogg's Corn Flakes advertisements. But I had heard Dad criticizing Senator McCarthy's warpath for Communists, especially those in the government.

Mimicking Dad, I asked my teacher, Sister Joan, "Is it right for Senator McCarthy to call so many people 'Commies'?"

"The senator is simply against Communists like the Church is," she said.

Pushing it further and repeating what I'd heard Dad say, "Did that make it OK for General Franco in Spain to use Nazi help to defeat the Communists?"

Sister Joan moved on without answering me.

After lunch she took me aside.

"Jimmie, I am surprised that you spoke so harshly about the senator."

I didn't answer. First, I looked at the silver cross that shone brightly against the black front of her habit. Then I looked at my shoes.

"I hope as you get older," she said, "you will more carefully develop your opinions."

"Yes, Sister."

I think she might have bawled me out if my mother didn't help the nuns by running errands for them and driving them to appointments. I did learn that putting a United States senator, the Catholic leader of Spain, and the Nazis in the same boat was going too far. I was supposed to keep those opinions to myself or not have them at all.

While walking my paper route and tossing *The Shopping News* onto porches, I'd try to fit together what the Catechism said, what the sisters said, what Dad said, and now what I thought. At school I began to ask a few questions, often copycatting Dad. Most questions stayed quarantined. Inside me the confidence to speak up was strengthening along with my leg muscles, now carrying all 203 papers.

THE HAIRCUT

Since the third grade Mom always had given me the quarter to pay the barber. The barber was a short, thin man with a pencil mustache like the movie star Clark Gable. He didn't talk much to kids. For us, a look and a hand sign were talk enough. I think he saved his talking for men. One haircut when I was twelve sticks with me.

I'd walked by Shooty's and into his empty shop. That wasn't unusual, because I'd gotten used to his being next door when he didn't have a customer. "Next door" was Shooty's Tavern.

I'm sure he sat where he could see a customer coming or heard the jingle of the brass bell attached to the shop door. I sat down opposite the two black barber chairs and waited.

Within a minute or two, he came in. His white barber jacket made him look a doctor, except for its shine. I think it shined because it was rayon or nylon that hair didn't stick to. Without a word, he picked up a towel and flicked it at the chair to chase any hair lurking in the seams where the leather met the chrome frame. He looked over at me and, without a word, patted the seat—my signal to mount up. His breath always let me know he'd been nursing a beer.

One reason this day stands out was my being the only customer, a good sign that he'd take his time cutting my hair. I closed my eyes and drifted. My arms and legs unhinged. The electric clippers hummed around my ears. The teeth of his comb fingered my scalp. The rhythmic snip-snip of his scissors cut away the sense of time. I drifted into a place just on the edge of sleep. I don't know how long I was there, but somewhere in there I heard the slap-slap of his straightedge razor against the hard leather sharpening belt that hung from the back of the chair. Then far off I heard the whipping sound of his stubby brush lathering up the shaving cream. I felt his fingertips meringue the warm whiteness around my ears and along the line where my neck meets the hair at the back of my head. With a few smooth swipes, the steel edge whisked away the fuzz that must have been there. Soon I felt a warm moist towel take away the remnants of lather. The tonic gurgled as he shook it from the bottle. I inhaled its sweet smell and felt its coolness as his hands patted it along the path just cleared of lather. I didn't want the haircut to end. I didn't want to open my eyes.

Then a thought snapped me alert even more than the door's jingling bell that signaled a new customer: *These feelings are so enjoyable, they must be sinful.* I automatically dropped them into my quarantine.

FATHER KNELLEKEN

Newly ordained Father K, that's what we boys called him among ourselves, replaced the athletic Irish assistant pastor who had introduced us to soccer—the "real football," he'd say with his lilting accent. Father K wasn't much interested in sports but was always friendly. He frequently joined us at recess. He'd often stroll along the border sidewalk with each of his arms draped over the shoulders of boys in my class. I was too busy to walk around because I usually was playing basketball.

As an altar boy we didn't get to choose which Masses we served. We served what Father Beglin assigned us or we didn't serve at all. No one liked serving the 6:30 morning Mass, Monday through Saturday. Those early times were given to older altar boys like me. I was a seventh grader.

One windy March morning still chills me. I made sure to get to the church early. Dad often said, "It's better to be an hour early than a minute late." I knew that was an exaggeration, but still I was always early.

The celebrant priest and the altar boy (only one was needed at the first Mass because attendance was rarely more than ten) entered at the back of the Church by a rickety wooden stairway that went up to the sacristy level. A little after six I'd climbed the stairs and waited close to the door trying to avoid the chill. A few minutes later I saw a window shade glow brown on the second floor of the rectory. I knew it had to be Father K's room because assistant pastors were always assigned to say the early Mass. Shortly before 6:30 Father K hurried up the stairs toward me, his right hand searching for keys in the jacket over his cassock. Neither of us said a word as he aimed the key at the lock which was hard to find in the dark. With a click, we were in. He turned left into the sacristy to robe himself for Mass. I walked straight down the narrow passageway behind the wall of the sanctuary to a room the same size as the sacristy but not nearly as neat. There I put on a cassock and surplice.

On my way back to the sacristy, where the priest and altar boys always entered to start the Mass, I picked up the long wood-and-brass candle lighter to light the candles for Mass. As I came into the sacristy I turned my back to Father K and opened a cabinet for a match to light the taper. I felt Father's hand on my shoulder. He turned me toward him, wrapped his arms around me, and drew me close to kiss me on the lips. As I reflexively turned my head sideways his unshaven cheek brushed my cheek.

"I need to light the candles," I said as I wedged my left arm across my chest with enough outward pressure to separate us.

He didn't say a word, but turned and went over to put on the final vestment laid out by the nun sacristan the night before. The vestment was green. My hand trembled as I lit the taper before escaping into the sanctuary. Throughout Mass I remained on full alert. *What was Father K doing? I don't understand.* I couldn't imagine a grownup man, especially a priest, kissing another male on the lips.

After Mass a parishioner came into the sacristy to talk to Father K privately. I quickly doused the candles, pulled off the surplice, and hung up the cassock. I hurried out the door and down the stairs. I walked home fast still remembering the sandpaper rub of Father K's unshaven cheek against mine. The quarantine swallowed the incident so fast it was as if it had never happened.

CHAPTER 4

St. Edward Seminary

MAY DAY

The Catholic Church during the late forties made May Day as big a celebration as holy days like Easter. I suspect it throttled into high gear to overtake the Soviet Union's May Day. Because Mary was the Mother of Jesus and listened to our rosaries, who was better qualified than her to offset the "Red Menace"?

The annual march in honor of Mary, the Mother of God, took place at St. Edward Seminary, which sat on a promontory overlooking Lake Washington and North Seattle. Tall fir woods carpeted its property to the west and followed the slope to the waterline. The seminary grounds provided the staging area for all grade schools in the Diocese of Seattle to gather in celebration. Parents substituted the outing to St. Edward on the first Sunday of May for the usual Sunday drive.

I had participated in the May Day celebration since early grade school. Now as a seventh grader I marched as an altar boy for St. Catherine's parish. Each parish sent a troop of elementary school students. At the head walked a single altar boy carrying the parish banner mounted on an eight-foot pole, followed by several parish altar boys in their cassocks and surplices. Scores of girls and boys in school uniforms rounded out the parish representatives. After the passing of hundreds of marching grade-schoolers and the last parish, an eighth-grade girl solemnly walked beside a younger boy who carried a crown of flowers on a silk cushion. After their passing, scores of priests trudged by in their cassocks and lace surplices. Bishop Connelly in his red-trimmed cassock and skull cap marked the final piece of the procession. The entire parade took an hour or more to snake its way from its start in the parking lot and up the gravel road rimmed with overflow cars to the white marble statue of Mary. Beaming parents strained to see their son or daughter pass by while pre-school siblings wedged between the cars to admire church flags and catch sight of the bishop. When parents, children, priests, and the bishop had ringed themselves around the elevated statue of Mary, the girl in the white dress took the crown of flowers, mounted a step-ladder, and placed the crown of flowers on the head of the statue. Mary's crowning climaxed the afternoon as hundreds of Catholics sang, "O Mary, we crown thee with blossoms today. . . ." The singing and pageantry filled me with the warm comfort of being Catholic.

The spirit of the May Day celebration cast a halo over the tan brick walls of the seminary and pulled me toward St. Edward. What became clear to me during the following eighth-grade year was a new meaning to the answer to Question #6 in the Baltimore Catechism: "Why did God make you?" "God made me to know Him, to love Him, and to serve Him in this world" translated into entering the seminary in the ninth grade, after graduating from St. Catherine's. The seminary was the road to the priesthood. Realizing what I wanted to do was a lot like my knowing I wanted the *Shopping News* route. It just was there, felt right, and I just needed to convince Mom and Dad. By mid-year I told my parents I wanted to enter the seminary. They were quiet. I knew they were skeptical. I think they probably were waiting for me to get over the idea. But as long as I didn't hear a "No," I held on tight to the dream of entering the seminary. I did follow their request to take the entrance exam for Seattle Prep, where Ron had graduated the year before. Then, after my score on the exam won a scholarship, I still persisted in pleading my case to go to St. Edward. Mom and Dad gave in and said OK.

St. Edward Seminary

Entering St. Edward meant, of course, that I would be leaving home and living for the first time away from the family. Mom and Dad passed over in silence the financial hardship of paying the expensive tuition and room-and-board, which piled on top of Ron's expenses at the University of Washington.

Standing with my mother in line for registration and room assignment that first day at St. Edward, I turned to the towhead standing behind me and asked, "What grade school did you graduate from?" That question launched my first friendship at St. Edward. Although the other ninth-grader and I didn't get to room together (all freshmen were assigned to a room with a seminarian one year older), I did share classes with him: Latin, algebra, English, history, and religion.

St. Edward routines swept me into a new world, a minor league version of Columbus landing in the New World. Eating meals without talking certainly was different than chatting at the dinner table at home. Stranger still was getting undressed in front of others before stepping into a shower room to queue up for one of the eight showers. For the first time I saw the difference between the circumcised and the uncircumcised. Ending the day by a bell that signaled "lights out" took getting used to. Even washing clothes called for a special routine. Each week I packed my dirty laundry in a brown suitcase-size shipping box to send home to Mom to wash. At the time I never thought how

Mom, and all the other moms, felt about this chore. Above all, it was hard to imagine not going home or seeing my parents until Thanksgiving. It was only September.

Any problems were to be taken to Father Healy, who doubled as my freshman confessor/advisor and Latin teacher. He stood a few inches shorter than me, maybe five-feet-six, with red hair and glasses that struggled to stay on his button nose. He never seemed to smile. The look on his face made me wonder whether he had a stomach ache. He walked like the wind-up metal soldier I received on a birthday during the war.

He began our first private meeting by reviewing my studies, which were going well. Because Mom had alerted him to my history of rheumatic fever, he counseled me not to run too hard in touch football, which had quickly become my favorite sport. He never directly asked me whether I missed home. I didn't want to tell him about my tears after dinner when I walked alone outside and saw the lights of North Seattle signaling from across Lake Washington. On those walks I often wondered what Mom, Dad, and Ron were doing less than three miles away by a crow's flight. I missed Toby's excitement after my paper route. I wondered whether he missed me as much as I missed him. I tried to quarantine those thoughts and feelings, but they broke out several times.

The once-a-week Confession differed from traipsing after the nuns to church where we'd push and shove into pews before being funneled like gum balls, one at a time, into Confession with either Father Beglin or Father K. At St. Edward, we confessed once a week at night before 9:00 p.m. lights-out when the florescent overheads turned amber and the long hallway became a Halloween spook house. I lined up with others outside Father Healy's door with hopes of confessing my sins and asking for absolution before the halls darkened. Finding sins was an ongoing problem. At the time I didn't know what masturbation was and how it typically topped the sin chart for adolescent boys. My knowledge of that sin hid in the future. My most reliable sin was anger when playing football or the occasional talking during class.

During noon and evening meals, eating mediocre food competed with listening to a major seminarian read a religious book from the elevated pulpit in the dining hall. I was told both body and soul required nourishment. While I had no problem with appetite, I did have a problem satisfying it. I soon learned that servings at the eight-man table followed seniority, beginning with the oldest minor seminarians, sophomores in college. Ninth-graders like me held spot seven or eight. If our table could empty its serving platters fast enough and our server was fast enough, chances were about one in ten of getting a second serving. Unfortunately, the odds for success were accurate. Bread broken apart in a bowl, however, was an available resource, which I weighed down with sugar and a half glass of milk to satisfy my hunger.

The St. Edward's meal I remember the most was breakfast November 5, 1952. Memory locked it in not because I came away hungrier or more satisfied than usual, but because the reading that morning was not from the life of a saint but from the morning paper announcing Dwight D. Eisenhower had been elected president. The news ignited thoughts about how my parents took the news, as both were staunch Democrats who I knew had voted for Adlai Stevenson. Those thoughts trickled in until my wanting to be home with them broke over me like a wave.

THANKSGIVING

The day before Thanksgiving, Ron drove when he and Dad came to pick me up. Mom and Grandma stayed home to prepare dinner for the next day. I came into the house through the garage and into the basement where I put my box of dirty laundry next to the washing machine. Then I whistled for Toby. He scampered down the stairs barking all the way. He wouldn't quit. I had to pick him up to make him shush. Upstairs Mom's and Grandma's kisses triggered a deep at-home feeling that soaked right though my skin. It made perfect sense, given that being away for more than two months had been my longest separation from family ever. Thanksgiving Day and the rest of the week whirred and blurred by. On Sunday I said my night prayers back at St. Edward and stayed awake longer than usual before trailing off to sleep.

My returned laundry in the second week of December included a letter from Mom. She often sent at least a note inside the laundry box. She thought it was poor budgeting to use a three-cent stamp unnecessarily by sending a separate letter. She wrote that Toby had been poisoned and died. The veterinarian said Toby's stomach contained raw meat embedded with shards of glass that caused fatal internal bleeding. She and Dad suspected a neighbor who had complained about Toby's barking. "Accusing won't bring him back," she added.

I cried and prayed, even though I knew there wasn't a dog heaven. Toby's death stirred thoughts about my rheumatic fever, death, and God. Illness, an accident, or martyrdom can bring death and take me to God's judgment. I knew following my Catholic life would make me ready.

A BIND

The push to stay with God's calling at St. Edward fought against the pull of being home. When November gave way to December, I decided to talk with Father Healy about the struggle inside me. During study time after supper I knocked on his door and heard his muffled, "Come in." Sitting and facing him from in front of his desk contrasted with the usual confessional view of his back.

"How can I help you?" he asked.

"I've been feeling funny."

"Funny?"

"I mean I don't feel right, like I shouldn't be here."

"Have you been thinking about home?"

"Yes."

"That's natural. You've never been away from home this long, have you?"

"I've never been away from home before, never stayed overnight at anybody's house."

"I think you're homesick. A lot of boys here have those same feelings. But I also know the feelings will pass. You have to be on your guard against the devil putting bad thoughts in your head. Do you know what I mean?"

I really didn't know what he meant, but I saw his face harden when he said "the devil." He wanted my thoughts quarantined.

We both backed away from homesickness into my studies. He smiled when complimenting me in how well I was doing in Latin. That evening during study time I again felt a push-pull inside me as two sides began to form around the familiar answer to Question 6 of the Baltimore Catechism: "God made me to know Him, to love Him, and to serve Him in this world, and to be happy with Him forever in the next." Did knowing, loving, and serving God mean staying at St. Edward, or could I still know, love, and serve Him outside the seminary? I felt like a Ping-Pong ball my head and heart volleyed back and forth.

The night before my parents came to pick me up for Christmas break I again spoke to Father Healy about my not feeling right. I couldn't seem to find words which would make us both feel okay. After about fifteen minutes he leaned forward, elbows on the desk, eyes locked on mine, and said, "If you leave St. Edward, you will be making the biggest mistake of your life." I left Father Healy's room tangled in ropes of worry. It took months for me to recognize the guilt embedded in his words.

The next morning I followed Mom's instruction to bring all my clothes, both clean and dirty, which filled both my scarred leather suitcase and the laundry box. As I climbed into the backseat of the family '50 Ford, Mom said, "Be sure and bring all your things from your room." I quickly backtracked to retrieve the cigar box holding pencils, erasers, and my Esterbrook fountain pen. I had everything from the room except the seminary's textbooks standing upright on my desk.

After Dad slipped the car into low gear and was easing past the oak entrance doors to St. Edward, Mom said, "Jim, take a good look at the front doors, because you won't be coming back." Her firm deliberate tone flooded me with relief and reassurance, the kind I felt when Mom had stroked my forehead and eased me into sleep during the first days of rheumatic fever eight years before.

Christmas 1952 diluted the mixture of relief and guilt I felt over leaving the seminary. I knew both Mom and Dad had decided I would come home. They always made big decisions together. A few days later Mom told me she had felt my unhappiness at Thanksgiving and between the lines of letters I had written home.

"Your father and I think it's better for you to make such big decisions, like becoming a priest, when you are older."

I never told her Father Healy's words kept repeating like a phonograph record with a stuck needle, "If you leave St. Edward, you will be making the biggest mistake of your life." I couldn't keep those words in quarantine.

CHAPTER 5

Seattle Prep

ENTERING PREP

Self-conscious and awkward, I walked with Mom up the wide steps to aging red-bricked Seattle Prep. Several boys raced past us on the way to their 8:30 a.m. first class. We stepped inside the wood and glass front doors and climbed the worn gray marble stairs guiding us to the first-floor office. Inside we faced a crowd of students firing requests at a well-over-fifty, white-haired secretary with neon red lipstick and penciled eyebrows.

"Mrs. Perkins, I need an admission slip to get back into class."

"Mrs. Perkins, I need five lunch tickets."

She fielded requests like a Yankee shortstop calmly taking care of business or tossing an extra-base request to the vice-principal, Father Weissenberg. When our turn came, Mom stepped forward calmly and firmly saying, "I'm Mrs. Tracy. Last Friday I called and made an appointment to meet with Father McDonnell this morning."

Mrs. Perkins shot a sideways glance at the half-open door to her right, above which shone a small wooden plaque emblazoned with "Principal" in gold letters. She guided Mom and me past the counter into Father McDonnell's office. Seeing

Mom, the priest rose and stepped around his desk with an extended hand.

"Mrs. Tracy, how are you?"

Her handshake was accompanied with a cordial eye-to-eye look, the kind I imagined she delivered to a customer at Frederick & Nelson.

"I'm fine," she replied.

"And this is your son whom you spoke of on the phone," he said while looking sideways at me but not shaking my hand.

I scanned his black cassock with French-cuffed white-shirt sleeves peeking out of the arms. More noticeable were his high forehead, dark eyebrows, and penetrating eyes. His nose was "aquiline," a Latin-rooted adjective I would learn a few months later meant like the beak of an eagle. From Ron I'd learned this Jesuit was famous for fostering debate contests, imposing discipline, and a shrill whistle that froze all students within earshot into statues.

With just two sentences of small talk, he got down to the business of my admission to Prep by asking to see my report card from St. Edward. He didn't acknowledge that I had taken the Prep entrance exam the previous April and won a scholarship, but hadn't accepted it because I'd chosen to go to the diocesan seminary. Aware that money was tight, especially after my $350 half-year at St. Edward, I hoped that somehow the scholarship would come alive again. Mom was too proud to bring it up; I was too intimidated to mention it; Father McDonnell was too smart to remember it. I later learned this Jesuit principal often persuaded well-to-do parents of scholarship winners to pay tuition anyway, a pattern that helped keep Prep financially afloat.

After glancing at the four As and one B on my report card, Father McDonnell turned to me and said, "Very good, you'll be in class 1A."

With a formal shake of Mom's hand, he escorted us back to Mrs. Perkins, whom he told to have a 1A student come to the office to show me the way to class. And so began three-and-a-half years at "Prep," Seattle Preparatory School for Boys.

Catching Up

Getting into Prep was one thing; fitting in was another. Enrolled in 1A, I quickly realized that scores on the spring entrance exam had sorted students into A to D classes, like different-sized eggs into graded cartons. I soon learned my 1A classmates were smart, some very smart. My first 1A Latin class left me frightened and floating adrift in verb conjugations that St. Edward had not yet introduced. After class I worriedly explained my predicament to the teacher, Father Coughlin. He said he would help me catch up if I came to his office during afternoon study halls.

Father Coughlin was tall and thin, probably in his late fifties, with teeth that didn't look like they received regular visits from a toothbrush. His hypnotic sing-song pattern of talking made it hard to keep my eyes open in class. When I came to his office for my first catch-up session, he had me sit next to him on his left with Henle's Latin grammar open on the desk in front of us. He patiently and clearly explained the tenses and pointed out what I needed to memorize. I felt comfortable until he shoved his left hand between my belt and denims. A couple of times he slipped four fingers between my pants and my tucked-in shirt but always with his thumb on my belt. At first I thought he might think I was going to run away, and he had to keep me in the chair.

Father Coughlin's hand moves brought a fleeting image of Father Knelleken. My fear of not catching up in Latin and the yellow light of "something's not right here" accelerated my mastery of Latin verbs after only a few private sessions. While this Jesuit's hand never wandered further than my hip, I knew why some students called him "Father Fingers." Once again, I automatically quarantined the incident. Repression ruled.

Formal sex education never came up in my Catholic schooling. At St. Catherine's a few times I became aware of the pleasant feeling of arousal while looking at bare-breasted African women in *The National Geographic.* Mom never explained sex beyond her hand motions when I was in the second grade and neither Dad nor the nuns touched the subject. Ron never said anything either.

A glimmer of sex came during my first Confession at Prep. After I had itemized my sins, the priest asked through the veiled grate, "Is there anything else?" and my saying, "No." Then he added, "No self-abuse?" Puzzled and curious, I said, "No," because I still didn't know what masturbation was and how it worked. I do remember him saying, "Very good."

GETTING STARTED

After catching up with my classmates in Latin, I began to feel comfortable in class, although I didn't raise my hand much. Algebra came easily, along with religion. The layman who taught Washington State History read from his notes and lulled many of us to the edge of sleep. The Jesuit priest who taught English late in the day pushed us hard. He expected accurate grammar, vivid verbs, and coherent structure. Only a few times did I earn an A on an essay.

Getting to know others was tough. Only one other St. Catherine's graduate had made the 1A class and we had never been close friends. During my first week no one said "Hi" or invited me to sit with their group at lunch. At the start of the second week I spotted two 1A students eating lunch together at an uncrowded table. I forced myself to go over and say, "Can I sit and eat lunch with you?" One returned "Sure," the other's look teetered on the edge of a smile. My relaxing exhale and the conversation that followed marked my first step into the web of social networks that laced Prep students together.

During those first months back home, Mom and Dad never brought up "St. Edward" beyond Mom's short explanation for removing me. They acted as if I hadn't been there. It's not that I wanted to talk about it, but their silence seemed odd. Ron didn't talk about the seminary either. He did seem to know I was struggling with something more than fitting in at Prep. No one knew how often the words of Father Healy about "the biggest mistake of my life" invaded my solitary time and brought me to tears.

Without asking me, Ron lobbied his college friends with whom he played basketball on weekends to let me join their games even though I was only fourteen. I wasn't big enough to grab many rebounds, but was able to score a few points. My inclusion in those games comforted me as much as my holding him around the waist when he took me riding on his bike years before.

By April of 1953 the move from St. Edward to Prep felt firm, like my grip on the baton passed to me in the relay I ran in freshman track. Running track and the hubbub of Prep activity dampened my guilt and dried up the tears.

FOOTBALL

With end of the school year, I thought ahead to the fall and to my dream of playing varsity football. At 145 pounds and six-feet tall, my light weight loomed as a major challenge. Physical education had never been part of Catholic schooling, and rheumatic fever had basically stopped exercise and playing of any kind for five years. No surprise that I was skinny. And Dad's slim genes didn't help my build either.

In searching for an answer to my weight problem, I learned from Jerry, a graduate of St. Catherine's one year ahead of me, that there was a gym in the University District where he conditioned for football. He led me to believe that weight-lifting and drinking the supplements sold at the gym would bulk me up. Although I'd given up the paper route before going to St. Edward, I averaged $2.25 each week from mowing lawns. I knew I could pay the gym fee of six dollars a month. I signed up. I tried camouflaging my thin frame from the body builders by wearing a loose-fitting sweatshirt and sweat-pants. Masking my build in the steamy sauna after working out was impossible. I knew it didn't make sense for me to go into that sweatbox after exercising when I was trying to gain weight, but that was the routine. All routines were soft rules that needed to be followed. The twice-a-day powders mixed with milk tasted like chalk and made Lenten sacrifices seem easy. Every workout ended with my weighing in and hoping for another pound.

On an August Monday 1953 I stepped forward naked for the football physical examination. I tried not to flinch when the doctor placed his cold stethoscope on my chest. I hoped shallow breathing would mask any heart murmur that's routinely packaged with rheumatic fever. Whether the backwash sounds of blood leaking back into the heart really wasn't there or whether he was distracted by the long waiting line behind me, the good doctor passed me. I had trouble containing the hallelujah inside me.

I quickly learned I liked—really liked—the electric shock that shot through my body with a solid tackle or a block that knocked down another player. I was one of the few who looked forward to tackling drills. And I came to realize my power came from legs developed over the three years of carrying the 203 copies of *The Shopping News*.

John Goodwin, the head football coach, was a stocky veteran of World War II who had played on one of the last football teams fielded by Gonzaga College. He was tough, intimidating, and subtly encouraging. He rarely praised us in a rah-rah way but would signal his approval with a single word or a quick glance. With me, a sophomore who had not played as a freshman, now vying for a third-string varsity position, he ordered me over the ball at center to hike and block.

After I'd kept other sophomores from getting by my blocks, he yelled, "Ditore, get over here." John Ditore was a 190-pound senior all-league lineman.

"Let's see whether you can get past this 'soph-o-more' who wants to be on the varsity," he added.

Unshaven Ditore lined up with his dark Italian eyes peering through me. Three times I heard Coach Goodwin bark, "Hike." The first time I was driven straight into the ground without getting my shoulder close to his body. The second time I was able to get one shoulder into his waist before he tossed me aside. The third time I was able to stay engaged with him until Coach Goodwin blew his whistle. The next day, when I looked at the list of varsity players traveling to Yakima to play Marquette in the first game of the season, I found my name, along with two other sophomores.

At the end of the season, I was disappointed at not playing in enough quarters to earn a varsity letter. Only the star sophomore, Ollie Flor, won a letter and the right to wear a letterman's sweater. Encouraging words like, "You did well and are on your way as a football player for Seattle Prep," helped a little—just a little.

JESUITS

During my sophomore year the differences between Jesuit scholastics and Jesuit priests caught my attention. The scholastics were only part-way through their priestly studies. Most scholastics were just ten years older than the students they taught. They smiled more, laughed more, and joked more, while the priests stood stiffer and more aloof.

Growing confident during the second semester—cocky, really—I stretched the limits of a fresh Jesuit scholastic assigned to Prep for student teaching. Assuming he hadn't learned our names yet, during roll-call I traded names with Terry Thompson. I failed, however, to take into account the change of identity would make me the first to say "Here" to "Thompson," a name alphabetically before "Tracy." Unfortunately the scholastic knew my name. He slowly repeated "Thompson" twice; each time I replied, "Here." The class grew quiet. The Jesuit met my smart-aleck joke by kicking me out of class. With nowhere in the stark hallway to hide for the remainder of the class period, I was soon approached by Father Weissenberg, the patrolling vice-principal.

"Tracy, why are you out in the hall?"

My frank admission led to his ordering me to follow him down to the basement boiler room, where heavy fuel oil fumes and dim light greeted me. Like a dentist who doesn't brandish the needle until just before the injection, he belatedly produced his sturdy wooden paddle as he said, "Grab your ankles." Three stinging swats brought my behind alive with a burning sensation I'd never felt before.

He ended our meeting with, "And you *will* answer to *your* name when called from now on, won't you?"

"Yes, Father."

Father Weissenberg's physical discipline fell in line behind the mental discipline Jesuits championed, and underscored my failure as a comic.

Father Menard, who taught us religion, exuded unshakeable Catholic faith, which left no room for questions or doubts. He strode up and down between the five rows of desks, his index finger and pumping arm popping imaginary balloons in the air as he made doctrinal points. His cassock with its extra wide cincture became a blur of black as his quick strides matched the thoughts tumbling out of him. Some of us tracked his up-and-down path; others, with heads down, doodled; other heads wobbled on the edge of a siesta. None of us doubted his faith in Mother Church or his eagerness for us to feel in tune with her authority.

But authority grated. Phrases like "blind faith" and "the Church has decreed" raised my hackles. Over time I wondered whether I had inherited from Dad his chafing at the heavy hand of those in charge at the railroad. My reflex against authority eventually surfaced. Having heard enough from Father Menard about how the Catholic Church shined in the world as a beacon of wisdom, I raised my hand to ask a question. What came out was a statement.

"Father, I don't think the Church's treatment of Galileo was right," I said.

That torpedo at the battleship of the Jesuit's faith raised his eyebrows.

"I think you always need to take Church actions in context," he responded.

"What 'context' includes condemning science?" I countered.

A dismissive smile followed, with an answer I can't recall. I do remember concluding that he had not addressed my question.

That brief exchange led me to ask Ron to take me along to Suzzallo Library on the U of W campus. Some Jesuit teachers would sarcastically refer to the U of W as the "pagan fishbowl" we could see across Portage Bay from Prep.

I marveled at the Suzzallo's reading room. The vaulted ceiling reminded me of a church. It draped lamps at the end of long chains over polished wooden tables that could have been set for banquets in medieval castles. The walls were lined with shelves of reference books and periodicals that rose to eight feet. And the silence made me hold my breath. I heard only the occasional scraping of a chair as a student rose and moved to retrieve a book or periodical. With altar-boy care, I began to find articles on Galileo and jot notes on three-by-five cards.

Armed with my newly found references, neatly ordered like so many cartridges in a gun belt, I re-engaged Father Menard. I presented evidence for my case that the Church was unfair to Galileo.

"Where did you get that information?" he asked.

With reference cards in hand I began my litany of citations from journals and encyclopedias, only to be interrupted with, "Those are not adequate."

"What *is* adequate?" I asked.

"*The Catholic Encyclopedia*," he answered. And with those three words he trumped my sources and ended the exchange while several of my classmates shot me the would-you-just-shut-up look.

I couldn't just shut up. Stuffing my anger, I spent the next few days trolling for a rebuttal. I went to the Prep library and found *The Catholic Encyclopedia*—not a single volume, but several hefty 10-by-14 inch tomes encased in aging black leather with gold lettering. I opened one volume and read. In the midst of an article on Galileo I found a brief reference to a society opposed to the Church and supportive of the maverick astronomer. I'd found a pearl.

The next day, just after lunch and before religion class, I went to the library and asked the unsuspecting Jesuit scholastic in charge if I could take one volume of *The Catholic Encyclopedia* to class for a project. Lugging the heavy tome under my arm, I hurried to the classroom a few minutes early to slip it on top of the books beneath my seat.

Part way through class I finessed a re-opening of the Galileo case.

"Father, do you think the Church could have been influenced against Galileo because he was supported by a society that was critical of the Church?"

"Well, I suppose that might have some influence," he responded, "if there *were* such a society."

"But there was such a society," I said.

"What is your source?" he fired back.

Reaching down I pulled out the heavy black trump card. "*The Catholic Encyclopedia*," I said.

The bell rang. Class ended. I filed out of the classroom, which never heard a reference to Galileo again.

TAUGHT ANOTHER LESSON

After lackluster grades in the first semester, four Bs and one A, Mom and Dad's silent review of my report card signaled their disappointment. I resolved to get straight As the second semester. This resolve emerged at the same time as I began counter-punching snide remarks some Jesuits made in class about the University of Washington, Ron's school. I took their comments personally as if a criticism of the U of W was in some way an attack on my family. I knew my folks couldn't afford to send Ron to Seattle University, the private Jesuit University. Hence, when an opportunity presented itself, I'd tout the superiority in academics and athletics of the U of W over those of Seattle U. I remember Mr. Fairhurst's eyes narrowing after one of my sarcastic exchanges with another student in his Latin class.

Mr. Fairhurst was a giant Jesuit scholastic standing six-feet-five and must have weighed well over 250 pounds. In addition to teaching, he had helped coach football, where he would stop drills to issue a stiff reprimand when he heard a reflexive "hell" or "damn" following a painful hit. He carried the same no-nonsense attitude into class.

Prep's grading system used only semester grades to calculate the official grade point, but did generate report cards every six weeks to let students and parents alike know where progress stood. My first two six-week report cards came with all As. Heading into semester finals I felt on my way to achieving my goal of straight As. The final exams were tougher than I had expected, but I felt my consistent performance would carry the day. My heart raced as I opened the envelope holding my semester grades—three As and two Bs. I felt punched.

I was baffled by the B in English and wanted to ask Mr. Fairhurst why the B in Latin. Before school ended for the summer, I hung back in his classroom until just he and I were there alone.

Reading my mind, he looked up from his desk and volunteered, "I could have given you an A because you were close enough. But in talking with your English teacher we thought you needed to learn that Jesuit academics are as good as any others."

Feeling the injustice of his words and the shock that two Jesuits would act that way, I couldn't utter a word. Awash in hurt feelings, I walked out of the classroom. There hardened within me a resolve never again to strive for perfect grades, a resolve I kept for the rest of high school. Only the passage of years made me realize that irritating remarks got under the skin of men of the cloth.

UPSWING

The school year at Prep always ended with student body elections that selected two juniors and one sophomore as officers for the following school year. I was surprised when Jerry, who had given me the gym tip for getting ready for football, and his brother Tom, both in the class ahead of me, asked whether I wanted to run on their ticket for school officers: Jerry for president, Tom for vice-president, and me for secretary-treasurer. I agreed. Because we didn't think enough students knew who we were, we blitzed the school with posters and painted our names on classroom windows. I don't recall giving a speech in front of the student body, but along with every other candidate for office I'm sure I did.

When I saw the sign on the bulletin board listing me as winning secretary-treasurer, I stood frozen in an unbelieving quiet space. I fought off guilt when I saw that both Tom and Jerry had lost. The letdown of failing to get all As followed by the upswing of winning the election made finishing sophomore year the final loop in a roller-coaster ride.

A JOB

You'd better get on the stick.

You can't get what you want sitting on your fanny.

Those thoughts prodded me to start looking for a job. I needed to take advantage of Prep's school year ending a few weeks ahead of the public schools. Procrastination meant I'd face more competitors for summer jobs. And I wanted a real job, one better than mowing neighbors' lawns, because in July I'd turn sixteen—driver's-license time. And driving required a car and gas.

Without either of us telling our parents, Ron had taught me to drive. In April he even let me cruise solo in his car. The years between us were shrinking. We both knew his '41 Dodge with its dented fenders and upholstery speckled with vinyl patches was not cool. We agreed that if I got a job and saved enough money to match what he got for selling the Dodge, we'd buy a better car together. Our agreement launched me on a mission.

"Even if you just want to be a dishwasher, you have to be sixteen to get a card from the restaurant workers union to work."

That's the abrupt response I got from the balding, chubby fellow at the downtown union office. As I marched back to the bus stop, I decided I'd deal with age once I had a job prospect. Because the University District was a short bus ride from home, I chose 45th and University Way as the hub of my search. From there, I'd job hunt businesses north, south, east, and west with my six-word question, "Do you have any job openings?" First came Bartell Drugs, then Nordstrom clothing store. Blood rushed to my face and my breathing got shallow at the "No" or "Not right now" that greeted my first several attempts. By late morning, the rejections had washed the self-conscious flush out of my cheeks. I was learning to steel myself to rejection and deliver a "Thank you" before moving to the next prospect.

After covering three blocks north and south on University Way, I started west on 45th. One block brought me to the Edmond Meany Hotel, the tallest building north of downtown. I was looking up at its sixteen stories when the steep slope of 45th made me brace myself and slow my stride. In front of me, a small group of adults had queued into a side entrance to the hotel. When I reached that spot, I read on the glass door "Edmond Meany Coffee Shop."

Go for it! propelled me forward. I edged my way through a line of lunch goers. The harried, middle-aged hostess was holding several menus in her hand and about to seat a party of six when I delivered my stock question. She hesitated as if I'd cast a spell over her. Instantly I realized how badly my question fit her dealing with the mayhem of the lunch rush. She gave me an angled look like a robin on the lawn listening for a worm. To my surprise she quietly said, "Come back at three o'clock," then turned away to seat the waiting six. Our exchange didn't fill ten seconds.

When I returned, just a few mid-afternoon customers were scattered among the side booths. The hostess was sitting at a table behind the cash register smoking a cigarette. She explained that increased business called for another busboy. I later learned that a Shriners convention had filled the hotel with a hard-drinking and big-spending clientele. She told me to come back the next morning at ten, after the breakfast rush, and learn how to bus dishes. If that went well, I'd have a job.

The next morning, Jimmy, a Japanese student at the U of W who was the most experienced busboy, quietly and always with a smile, gave me a 30-minute beginner's lesson in bussing. I thought of Ray Ishii and my resolve years before never to let the word "Jap" escape my lips. Here was a young non-American Japanese, whose relatives probably did kill Americans, teaching me something I needed to know.

"It's okay to use two hands when starting out," he said. He showed me how to heft a 30-inch tray loaded with dirty dishes from waist level to a few inches above my right shoulder, right hand on the bottom, left hand gripping the outer edge.

"You try it," he said.

The tray dipped and rocked as I slowly raised the tray.

"Your left hand will keep the tray level until your right hand learns to feel the weight." He smiled and nodded as I practiced several lifts.

Next he had me walk the loaded tray across the kitchen.

"Don't look at the tray; look where you're going. Your hands will know how to keep the tray level."

After our session, Jimmy told the hostess I would do fine. She sent me upstairs to get employee papers to be filled out and returned the next morning. Glancing over the papers on the bus ride home, my eyes locked on two items: "Date of birth" and "Age." My sixteenth birthday was six weeks off. How could I not lie and still get the job? In wrestling with this dilemma I recalled the execution of priests in England after Henry VIII broke with the Catholic Church in the 1500s. When the king's men came to the homes of Catholics and asked, "Are you harboring a priest?" or "Is there a priest in your home?" the Jesuits had reasoned and advised that Catholics could answer "No" and not be lying because the real question was, "Are you harboring a priest who must die by order of the king?"

Age was a tougher nut to crack. Using Jesuitical reasoning, I decided to accurately put down my birthdate, including the year 1938. Because it was now 1954, I hoped the bookkeeper would do simple mental subtraction and come up with sixteen without noticing the months. Then a workaround popped into mind: a baby of ten months is not called a one-year-old, but is in its first year; I am fifteen but am in my sixteenth year. Using that foot-loose logic, I filled in 16 for age. Deep down I knew that was a stretch, but I really wanted the job.

As I handed in my paperwork the next morning, I noticed how my sweaty hands had warped the first page. The bookkeeper scanned the application. He looked up and said, "Everything looks fine." And he never mentioned any need for a card from the union. I smiled and kept the *Hallelujah!* to myself.

Within a week, I'd graduated to just one hand, palm and fingers spread wide on the bottom of the heavy trays, balancing and pumping them six to twelve inches above my shoulder. The pinnacle of bussing came later when I could tango through a crowd with just four extended fingers and the thumb balancing twenty-five pounds of dishes above everyone's head.

MAUREEN

The time clock, where I punched in and out for every shift, hung on the wall in the kitchen for the posh dining room, the Marine Room, a floor above the coffee shop. While punching out after a shift in early July, I caught sight of Maureen.

Maureen walked with a natural sway to her hips that was hard to see in the black skirt that fell below her knees, but my eye for detail noticed it right away. The work uniform she wore consisted of two suspender-like straps over the shoulders of a long-sleeved white blouse that met two buttons at the waist of the skirt. The outfit was supposed to blend well with the starched black dresses worn by the waitresses Maureen helped in the dining room. Her title was "water girl," the perfect description for a sixteen-year-old blonde who looked like she stepped off a Dutch Cleanser label. Her subtle sexy walk hypnotized me even more when I was sent upstairs to the dining room as a substitute busboy.

How do I get to know her? After overhearing short exchanges between Maureen and Marie, who worked in the salad pantry, I figured out they were sisters. With careful listening I pieced together the bigger picture. Maureen, the teenager, lived with her married sister, who guarded her like a protective mother.

My chance came early in August while waiting at the chest-high shelf separating the pantry work area from the aisle where waitresses came by to pick up their orders. I was ready to carry out the rush order of crab cocktails Marie was deftly assembling. Maureen was helping her sister and together they choreographed crabmeat, celery, crab legs, and cocktail sauce into mounds inside a chilled goblet. Without slowing their fast-moving hands, they chatted quietly. I listened in to their subdued exchange.

"The hostess asked me to work late," Maureen said.

"I hate to ask Rick to come all the way back to pick you up later," Marie responded. "He's already in the car with the kids waiting for me to get off shift in fifteen minutes."

My mid-July driver's license and having Ron's car today led me to interject, "I'm working late too and could drive Maureen home."

Marie's dark eyes looked up at me and then shot a glance sideways at Maureen.

Maureen returned her sister's look with a placid look and, "That could work."

Marie stamped her approval on the first Maureen-Jim private time together with, "Then you would be home tonight around 9:30."

Maureen was quiet, but we chatted at work when time allowed. And by late in the month she was able to carry her part of our lengthening telephone conversations. Her disposition was sweet and never angry. Why she lived 150 miles away from her mother was a mystery to me, one that I felt was too sensitive to touch. I figured out her parents were separated because her father had a problem with alcohol. Her folks weren't divorced, because her mother was a good Catholic.

After I took Maureen out on our first date in the Dodge, I pressured Ron to buy the perfect car I'd found, a dark-blue two-door '47 Ford. The sum of what I had saved plus what he could get for selling his clunker closed the deal. Within two weeks Ron and I were sharing the Ford.

July and August 1954 pumped me full of excitement that comes with first-time triumphs—pocketing paychecks from a real job, driving a car, and dating a pretty blonde. Every morning I awoke with an energy that popped me out of bed. Summer momentum carried me toward September's football and return to Prep.

INTRIGUING JESUITS

Junior year also brought new classes and new teachers. During the previous year-and-a-half I had learned that Jesuits all marched under the banner of St. Ignatius, but their steps varied. I'd felt understood by a few and burned by a few. I measured my new teachers carefully. Mr. Reilly, the scholastic teaching junior English, stood slim, handsome, and hard to figure out. The story circulated that he had been a young Army recruit in World War II who had fought in the Battle of the Bulge, the bloodiest battle of the war for Americans. American casualties against the Nazis totaled 89,000—19,000 killed, 47,000 wounded, and 23,000 missing. Another story related that the previous year Mr. Reilly had unraveled in tremors and sweat when a prankster set off a firecracker behind him.

In class, Mr. Reilly's look could shift from neutral to serious with a quick glance, while a twinkle and a budding smile could lighten the classroom in an instant. And what he said about grades often didn't sound teacher-like or religious—"If you don't give a damn, I don't give a damn."

He followed the Jesuit tradition of memory assignments. The Order acted as if memory was a muscle requiring daily exercise, either in Latin or English or both. As an English teacher, Mr. Reilly always assigned a poem to memorize. At the beginning of each class he would call on one student to stand and begin to recite the poem out loud. To keep us alert, he'd point to another student mid-poem to take over and continue. Some of the poems he chose stirred my curiosity. *Why did he pick this one? How does that fit with being a Catholic, let alone a Jesuit?*

His spiritual side, I thought, guided his choosing *High Flight*, a poem by John Gillespie Magee, Jr., a young American serving in the Royal Air Force. After completing the challenge of flying his English Spitfire to an altitude of 33,000 feet, Magee wrote:

High Flight

Oh! I have slipped the surly bonds of earth
And danced the skies on laughter-silvered wings;
Sunward I've climbed, and joined the tumbling mirth
Of sun-split clouds - and done a hundred things
You have not dreamed of - wheeled and soared and swung
High in the sunlit silence. Hov'ring there
I've chased the shouting wind along, and flung
My eager craft through footless halls of air.
Up, up the long delirious, burning blue,
I've topped the windswept heights with easy grace
Where never lark, or even eagle flew -
And, while with silent lifting mind I've trod
The high untrespassed sanctity of space,
Put out my hand and touched the face of God.

Magee died in 1941 at the age of nineteen in a mid-air collision during training in England. I wondered whether Mr. Reilly felt a connection with Magee—both were Americans in World War II and both danced with death. Both had a spiritual side that probably helped them cope with the prospect of death. I also realized they both were just two or three years older than me when they ran the gauntlet of war. Or was this Jesuit reminding us of the nearness of war? The Korean War had ended less than six months before.

And I can still hear Mr. Reilly calling out, "Tracy, *Richard Cory.*"

Richard Cory

Whenever Richard Cory went down town,
We people on the pavement looked at him:

He was a gentleman from sole to crown,
Clean favored, and imperially slim.

And he was always quietly arrayed,
And he was always human when he talked;
But still he fluttered pulses when he said,
"Good-morning," and he glittered when he walked.

And he was rich—yes, richer than a king,
And admirably schooled in every grace:
In fine, we thought that he was everything
To make us wish that we were in his place.

So on we worked, and waited for the light,
And went without the meat, and cursed the bread;
And Richard Cory, one calm summer night,
Went home and put a bullet through his head.

My mind always reeled when I reread the final line of Edwin Arlington Robinson's poem. I sensed Mr. Reilly had more in mind than the obvious folly of never assuming that what you see is the whole story. And though the Church had taught me suicide was a terrible sin, I thought it would be sinful to judge Richard Cory without knowing what he was thinking and feeling. I don't recall Mr. Reilly telling us his thoughts on the poem. He stood at ease, letting us discuss a poem's meaning without intruding. He was both a mystery and a model.

SINNING

My struggles with the Church began to flood my moral life. By the end of football season, Maureen and I had begun going steady. And, of course, we experimented with sex. Well, more bluntly, we sinned a lot. We limited ourselves to petting, because we both understood that intercourse could put us on a crash course with pregnancy. Condoms, of course, couldn't be considered, because they were against the "natural law" (whatever that was) and forbidden by the Church.

The quarantine inside me where I'd isolated troublesome experiences with Church teaching and churchmen took a new turn. Now I was trying to stuff away part of me, what I was doing. Guilt, like a jack-in-the-box, kept popping up. Attempts to obscure my sinfulness in the whirlwind of studying, working, confessing, attending Mass and taking Communion failed. A dull ache shadowed me.

I knew parts of my relationship with Maureen were good. In the spring of our junior year, when we both knew an unusual Catholic school holiday would slip by the notice of my parents and Maureen's sister, we planned an entire day for ourselves. We made our lunches at home as we always did and acted as if we were going to school. I dropped Ron at the U of W and Maureen caught her bus for Holy Rosary. I picked her up at the bus stop in Ballard near her school. I drove to the close-by Hiram Chittenden Government Locks, the "Ballard Locks" to most Seattleites. We walked the paths laced through the grassy slopes above the waterway. Maureen shared the dream of her mother and younger sister moving to Seattle where the three of them could live together as a family. I shared my fears of going to college and whether I really could become a doctor or a lawyer. Our talking flowed back and forth as easily as a playground swing. Stops punctuated our conversation where, hand-in-hand, we'd silently watch the steel gates open to usher in tugs and cabin cruisers for the passage from the salt water of Shishole Bay to the fresh water of Salmon Bay. We ate our sandwiches on a bench beneath a towering maple just beginning to re-leaf itself. Then we walked again. Saltwater air tinged with diesel exhaust from idling boats followed us. The outbound boat traffic made me think, but not say, our not knowing where the vessels were headed mirrored our not knowing where our future together would take us. That day still rests under the banner of good.

The weekly confession of my sins mixed relief and guilt and resisted quarantine. I didn't want to end the relationship, the devil's workshop as some priests would describe it. At one level I knew our sexual connection was deemed sinful, but I found it hard to believe a loving God would damn us to hell for eternity. Yet the clear teachings of the Church resided within me. I knew my thinking would be categorized as "rationalizing." Guilt was never far away.

"This young man, just about your age, was driving his girl-friend home. He was a good driver, didn't speed or run lights. Not more than thirty minutes before, he and his girlfriend had engaged in sexual acts. They had no reason to think a drunk driver would ignore a red light and kill them instantly." Long pause. "But that's what happened."

And that's how the visiting Jesuit opened my junior-year retreat, a boiled-down version of *The Spiritual Exercises* of St. Ignatius. Retreats lasted from Wednesday through Friday before Easter. Each day came with a lightened class load, attendance at Mass, and two forty-five-minute talks in the chapel that were aimed at scaring us and steering us down a more spiritual path.

I can't remember much about the retreats during my first two years at Prep when freshmen and sophomores were always grouped separately from the upper classmen. Testosterone levels probably would have made the same division. At fourteen and fifteen I didn't do much that was sinful. But now the priest was addressing me as a junior, mired in sin.

I knew well from grade-school Catechism the difference between an unforgiven venial and unforgiven mortal sin. The first got you sentenced to the fires of purgatory for a limited time; the second put you in hell for eternity. Eternity, like infinity, rekindled the "forever" that had made me dizzy during my rheumatic fever days.

If love of God didn't defer sex until marriage, then fear of hell might. And because I'd never heard of any sexual sin that wasn't mortal, I knew I was in deep trouble. I flashed back to St. Edward Seminary and Father Healy's dire prediction for leaving. I wondered whether the bind I found myself in was part of what he meant.

With the end of my junior year and the start of summer, I tried to outrun the growing shadow of conscience by plunging into extra hours at work and conditioning for fall football. When not working, I had spent as much time as possible with Maureen, whose dream of living as a family with her mom and sister had come true; in late August both moved from Yakima to West Seattle. There the three began living together in subsidized housing, a town house nested among many others the government had built during World War II.

Mrs. Kiser, Maureen's mother, with her swollen ankles, thickening torso, and graying hair, struck me as much older than my mom. Her smile puffed out dimpled cheeks below glasses that often slipped part way down her nose. The first time I met her she looked me up and down over the top of her glasses from her barely over five-foot frame. She spoke little then and little over the months that followed. She often acknowledged me with a neutral glance before slowly climbing the stairs to her bedroom, one of two on the second floor.

Mother and daughters lived together, although I don't recall them doing anything as a threesome, like fixing a meal. I saw two bubbly teenage daughters volunteering to shop for the groceries and asking, "What can I do to help?" Their eager words were often met with silence or a wan smile followed by,

"I think I will go upstairs and rest awhile." Maureen more than once said to me, "I wish Mom was happier." She never said it, but I knew her dream of a close family with her mother and sister was not to be.

My mom couldn't have contrasted more with Maureen's mom. Mom spoke up often, signaled disapproval with a look, emphasized education, and looked after her boys the way a she-bear protects her cubs. At the beginning of summer, Mom had begun underlining shortcomings she found in my relationship with Maureen. She was careful not to be too direct because by this time she recognized my resistance to authority. In line with her expectation that I would enter the U of W the following fall, she spoke about how important it was to develop relationships with people with comparable education. She knew Maureen had no plans for college. She made it clear on one occasion that any plans of marriage in college, if they should enter my smitten head, were impractical and certainly did not have a place in hers. Mom was not good at being subtle. She would say, "When you get to the university, you won't have time to drive to West Seattle."

The summer seemed to end just after it started. As a senior, I felt good about having been elected student body president in the spring, but even better about being elected co-captain on the football team in the fall. Both, however, only gave me more excuses to put off facing myself. Just as characters in a play can crowd on stage, my Catholic faith, my sinfulness, Maureen, questions about my abilities, and Mom's plans elbowed their way inside me.

MORE JESUITS
In 4A Latin and English I came to know Mr. Galbraith, a Jesuit scholastic in his second year of teaching. His high forehead

blended into a retreating hairline above rimless glasses like the ones Mom wore just after World War II before heavy dark rims became the rage. He'd often stand by the door or the window, book in hand, listening carefully to the answers we gave. His movement was liquid and never seemed rushed when he walked to the blackboard to dissect the grammar of a Cicero sentence. Even when he wrote quickly on the board and the motion of his arm stirred a mist of yellow chalk, the dust never seemed to cling to his neat black cassock as it often did with other Jesuits.

Mr. Galbraith sensed the swell of our final year carrying us to graduation. He gave us slack. But his quiet manner steered us back to the lesson at hand with a pause or a question, never with the quick jab of a raised voice some teachers used. I sensed he always kept one step ahead of us even when we fudged an answer or two during a quiz.

After football season was behind me and the second semester had begun, Mr. Galbraith jolted me with, "Tracy, why don't you enter the senior oratory contest? The winner represents the school in the Hearst Newspapers National Oratory contest."

"Isn't that for the guys in the debate club and speech contests who are used to speaking a lot in front of others?"

"As student body president, don't you talk to the whole student body and fire them up before all the big games? And you introduce outside speakers who come to address the whole school."

Prep winners the prior two years intimidated me most—one won the national contest in New York City, the other won the regional West Coast title and competed in the nationals. I knew the hurdles: first, the Prep contest, next Catholic state, then all state high schools, West Coast regional, and finally the national finale. To me it looked like climbing Mount Si, then Mount Rainer, and ultimately Mt. Everest. But I did make the varsity football team as a sophomore, although I didn't win a letter. Mr. Galbraith's suggestion stirred an itch to compete. His willingness to coach me brought my "Yes." I began working on what I thought was the less-than-exciting speech topic of John Adams, second president of the United States.

Mr. Galbraith, in his kind but firm way, insisted I begin by researching the life of John Adams. Then he required an outline. The outline led to the first of seven drafts that stiffened flabby structure and weeded out legless verbs. I trimmed away adjectives and adverbs. Mr. Galbraith never rewrote a single sentence. He would, however, make comments like, "This sentence is too long. Change the paragraph order in this section. Use stronger verbs that can touch the audience." After the eighth revision, he was satisfied with the writing. Then he met with me after the class day was done to coach speech delivery. He shepherded me through hours of practice. Like a maestro, he guided me to vary the emphasis, to make eye contact with specific individuals in an imagined audience, and above all to build a crescendo toward the end without cresting too early.

I didn't triumph at the national contest; I didn't conquer the West Coast; I didn't win the wider state contest either. I took second. Mr. Galbraith never mentioned my cresting too early in the state final, but we both knew. "If only I had" dogged me after learning the Franklin High School senior who took first place went on to win the national title. Above all, though, this Jesuit's patience, encouragement, and selfless support made all my effort worthwhile. He extended himself for me more than any other teacher or Jesuit.

A Way Out

"You might want to take a look at this," Dad said as he handed me a single mimeographed page.

We had just sat down at the kitchen table, one of the few days when our afternoon schedules overlapped, Dad home from work and me with just homework to do.

"What's it about?" I asked as I took the sheet.

"Take a minute to look it over and you'll know."

A quick read told me that the Great Northern Railroad was offering three college scholarships to children of employees. In addition, the company promised summer work during college.

"Why do you think they're offering the scholarships?" I said.

"I had the same question until I heard the scuttlebutt at work. Management wants to get young blood into the company. A lot of people think railroads will be replaced by airplanes. Can you imagine how many airplanes it would take to move the heavy load of a single boxcar, let alone a train with 100 cars?"

That night at dinner Mom chimed in.

"It says you need to fill out an application form and submit an essay. Then they'll choose three winners from the final six invited to Minneapolis for interviews. I think that's right up your alley."

The prospect of easing the financial load of both Ron and me at the university sparked a resolve that always came with competition, especially one where I felt I had a good chance of winning. I completed the application and typed up the essay after Mr. Galbraith had gone over it. Within ten days a three-cent stamp carried off my submission to Minneapolis.

Frank, a close classmate, had no worries about college. He could go to any college he wanted because he would grad-uate either as valedictorian or salutatorian and his parents were wealthy. Brains and money are a winning combination. The irony was that he had decided to enter the Jesuit Order, which had no tuition.

I was surprised when Frank matter-of-factly said he was go-ing to enter the Jesuits. I considered him a close friend: he was in most of my classes, we were both starters on the football team, and we double-dated together. His well-to-do parents always smiled and welcomed me into their three-story brick home in Madison Park. His surprising Jesuit choice let me know he was a lot more private than I was. My likes and dislikes too easily bubbled to the surface.

A few days after I had entered the scholarship competition, Frank told me he and three others were going to visit the Jesuit Novitiate at Sheridan, Oregon. He asked whether I would like to come along and share the driving. With curiosity and a chance to drive a new Oldsmobile convertible, I said "Yes."

A Jesuit scholastic arranged the visit and agreed to escort us to the isolated hive of Jesuit formation. Once there, Prep graduates who had entered the Jesuits would give us a tour, have lunch with us, and answer questions about their life in the Order. It sounded like a fun way to peek into the making of a Jesuit. Riding and driving over four-hundred miles round-trip in one day seemed worth it.

We left before 7:30 on a gray, drizzling Sunday morning. The Jesuit chaperone and two classmates accordioned themselves into the back seat. One other classmate and I filled out the front seat with Frank at the wheel. When traffic thinned out south of Tacoma, Frank kept a steady sixty-five, a speed that made the rain pelting the canvas top sound like we were sitting inside a bongo drum. In spite of the pitter-patter thumping I drifted off to sleep. The braking and sways of Frank's maneuvering through Portland traffic woke me up just after ten. We were about an hour from Sheridan.

High gray clouds floated above the hills buttressing the Yamhill Valley. Rain had taken a breather in Oregon. We caught sight of a two-story gray cement building sprawled across a hilltop a mile off Highway 18. A partial third-floor bulged up in the middle with a stark cross topping it off. We wound our way across bare farmland, then uphill through orchards of fruit trees. We passed a small herd of Holstein cows we'd soon learn provided milk for the Jesuit community. Finally, we crunched and squished over gravel and mud to a stop in a small parking area to the left of the Novitiate's front entrance.

I waited with the others inside the heavy oak front doors, all of us wide-eyed. I stared at a different, rather stark, picture of the Virgin Mary and the infant Jesus, both wearing oversized jeweled crowns—Madonna Della Strada (Our Lady of the Way, patroness of the Society of Jesus, I later learned).

The first young Jesuit to meet us was Gary, an acquaintance I'd played football with the previous year. He was now uniformed in a black cassock and Roman collar. His outfit triggered a double-take. If he weren't so young, you'd think he was a priest. Soon three other Prep graduates joined us. They guided us to the narthex, the area outside the chapel, where the floor glistened with faint three-foot circles left behind from a fresh buffing. A whiff of floor wax hung in the air. The chapel was the one place we were welcome to see; Jesuit living quarters within the cloistered areas remained closed to our secular eyes. This aura of secrecy added to Jesuit mystery. Yet, in spite of the restrictions on what we could see, we were granted enough time to talk in the visiting rooms and outside where the rain still restrained itself.

I became increasingly interested in the conversation between Frank and the Jesuits. Questions and answers ricocheted from how each day was spent to more personal ones, like whether any of them regretted not going to college as some of us planned. I listened as a spectator. I listened more. At some point, I became a participant who didn't speak. I'd never been part of a conversation in which I didn't talk. Time jetted by. At four o'clock, the Jesuits needed to return to their routine, probably Sunday benediction, and we knew we had a long drive back to Seattle.

During the drive back a gyro spun inside me. Each of the four Prep Jesuits struck me as quite different, ranging from athlete to scholar. What was never talked about, but what lingered most with me, was a peacefulness in each of them, as if they were standing on ground firmer than what was under my feet.

The backdraft following the visit to Sheridan pulled energy out of me and left me quiet and reflective over the next few days. I didn't talk much at dinner and I skipped calling Maureen, a rare event. The idealized purity of Sheridan contrasted with my chronic turmoil bouncing between low and high and never turning off. I thought of Gary and the other Prepsters-turned-Jesuits and the lives they were leading. When I thought of Jesuits, I thought of those I admired— Mr. Galbraith and Mr. Reilly. I looked at the Jesuit road as one that led away from sinfulness and toward a better life of self-sacrifice serving others. It offered a pure life, one immersed in serving the Catholicism I was steeped in.

The following Wednesday, I sat gazing at the black rotary phone. I shuffled my thoughts like a deck of cards, not knowing what I would say. Finally, I picked up the phone and dialed.

Within a minute of my saying, "Hi," Maureen asked, "What's wrong?"

I fumbled for words, finally saying, "I really was affected by my visit to Sheridan and it's got me thinking."

"Thinking about what?"

"What it would be like."

"Are you thinking you'd like to go there?" she asked.

"Yes, I think maybe I am."

With that short answer I heard her "Oh," and the drop in her voice.

I don't recall how long we continued to talk. Not long. A clumsy one-sided ending of a relationship, an ending that made me feel cruel. Yet, it felt like it was the right thing to do.

Easter 1956 fell on April Fools' Day, which meant the yearly Prep retreat would come a few days before and just a few weeks after the trip to Sheridan. Unlike the retreat the year before, this one did not vice me in the sinner-Catholic bind I'd suffered then. Even the melodramatic talks that zeroed in on "sins of the flesh" stung less. While Maureen and I had not completely ended our two-year relationship, both of us knew it was over.

With Mom I broached my interest in the Jesuits with passing comments, such as "Gary showed the same dedication in the Order that he used to show in football" and "The education the Jesuits go through really is thorough."

I knew Dad was still more inclined than Mom to respect my decisions. I was sure she envisioned me as a physician, an attorney, or a dentist like Ron would be, not as a Jesuit. While I had not announced my intention to enter the Order, the confusion which had been spinning inside me began to take shape like a lump of clay on a potter's wheel.

High School Graduate 1956

By early May, I'd decided to enter the Jesuits. With acceptance, I cancelled my scheduled interview for the Great Northern scholarship in Minneapolis and prepared for graduation at the end of the month.

I'm sure there was surprise, perhaps misgiving, among some Jesuits at Prep when they learned I had applied to enter the Order. I'm sure some viewed me as too much the maverick to fit into the Order. Whatever their reactions, they never shared them with me. For my part, I felt a calm resolve tinged with eagerness for the mid-August entry into the Jesuit Order.

CHAPTER 6

Novitiate

In July 1956 I received a letter from the Novitiate specifying acceptable clothing and personal items for those entering the Jesuits. The Order allowed only black pants to be worn beneath the black cassock. Black socks and black shoes would complete our day-to-day outfit. For outdoor work and athletic gear we could wear Levis, sweatshirts, and work boots or tennis shoes. Aftershave lotion, deodorants, and class rings were not acceptable. Alarm clocks, radios, and books also appeared on the do-not-bring list. The letter offered a choice of two arrival dates, August 15 or September 7.

I wanted to enter as soon as possible. Exhilaration drove that choice, imprinted with the Catechism goal of knowing, loving, and serving God. A tingling satisfaction ran through me, the kind that comes with solving a complex math problem, but many times stronger. The solution was perfect: the Church opens the avenue to God; within the Church the Jesuit Order offered me an elite niche where as a priest I will serve God. In addition, the celibate life of a priest solved the problems of sinfulness and guilt that had tormented me.

ARRIVING AT SHERIDAN

The acceptance letter ended with directions to Sheridan, a small town in the heart of Oregon's Yamhill Valley. This rural town took its name from Civil War General Philip Sheridan, who as a young lieutenant commanded Fort Yamhill. The lieutenant worked his way up the military ladder until he accompanied General Grant to Appomattox to accept the surrender of Confederate General Robert E. Lee. The military history of the valley fit well with the Jesuits establishing a Novitiate there in 1931, a boot camp for those entering the Order. I soon came to know that the Order's training echoed General Sheridan's military background.

Dad and I shared the driving to Sheridan with Mom, unusually quiet, riding in the back seat. Like the good railroad worker he was, Dad carefully noted the route and the time it took between cities. I was sure he wanted to have an accurate estimate of travel time for their return visits—no more than one every three months was permitted. Visits home were not permitted, except for family emergencies.

After winding up the road to the Novitiate and parking in a graveled spot, the three of us made our way through the heavy oak front doors. Inside, we faced a mingling group of parents dropping off their sons. Father Elliott, the overseer of novices, walked over and introduced himself to my parents and me. He stood over six-feet tall, about the same height as Dad. His black cassock hung on his thin sixty-year-old frame and stopped just above high-top dress shoes that looked like those my Grandpa Dan wore the few times I had visited him. Wire-rimmed glasses framed his eyes and drew attention to one drooping eyelid. All my observations added up to "quietly intimidating."

He told my parents I'd be shown where to put my belongings and they were free to have some refreshments in the visitors' room. A novice, who had been shadow-walking behind Father Elliott and obviously had heard my name during the introductions, waved another novice forward. I felt as if I were being handed off in a carefully choreographed dance.

This second novice stuck out his hand, saying with a smile, "I'm Brother Ellis. I'm in my second year here and I've been assigned to help you get settled. While your parents are meeting other parents, let's start by getting your bags up to your cubicle."

On the way to the car for my two suitcases, Brother Ellis explained how each novice is addressed as "Brother" and a "cubicle" is the equivalent of a room where a novice prayed, studied, and slept.

"For the first eight days I'm called your 'guardian angel,' which means I'm supposed to explain the routine, like calling each other 'Brother.' You're free to ask me questions."

I was in an absorbing phase, just trying to soak up the lingo and not make a mistake. We lugged my suitcases to a second-floor dormitory room beehived with eight identical "cubicles," ten-by-six-foot enclosures. Mine was the second one to the left of the single entrance. Seven-foot-high wood partitions separated my cubicle from those on each side. A brown canvas curtain, bunched tight on a wire at the cubicle's open end, provided the necessary privacy to change clothes or sleep. We plopped the suitcases on the Army-surplus bed. My scan took in a small wooden desk with its single middle drawer. A small curtained bookcase stood opposite the desk. Brother Ellis said it served as a clothes bureau. A prie-dieu, a wooden kneeling bench fitted with a raised armrest, completed the bare-bones furnishings. This living quarter was starker than the room I'd shared with another seminarian at St. Edward four years before. I didn't mind. Living quarters had never crossed my mind as important. I was here to live a higher-order life in the best way I could.

We returned to the visitors' parlor where I found Dad standing next to Mom, who was chatting with another lady. Dad never liked small talk with strangers. Mom excelled at it. Seeing me, Mom broke off her conversation. Dad looked at his watch, then at Mom and said, "It's a long drive back. It's time for us to get on the road."

The Jesuit Novitiate, Sheridan, Oregon
(Jesuit Oregon Province Archives)

We walked down the sandstone steps and across the graveled roundabout to my parents' '53 Pontiac. My decision to enter the Jesuits hung in the air. I'd never told them all the reasons underpinning that choice. I'm sure they pieced together my desire to serve the Church in the best way I knew, as a priest. But I'm sure they weren't aware of my resolve to escape the sinfulness felt for the past two years. Neither Dad nor Mom ever challenged my choice, although I suspect Dad had discouraged Mom from voicing her objections. Right then Mom maintained the eerie quiet she'd kept on the ride down. She avoided eye contact. I wondered whether she wanted to spirit me away as she had at St. Edward, a move I welcomed then. Today was entirely different.

Dad stood back after opening the passenger door for Mom. She pivoted and gave me a quick hug, a peck on the cheek, and, without a word, slipped into the front seat. She looked straight ahead. I suspect she was holding back tears, a rare visitor for her. I walked with Dad around to the driver's side where our hands met in a handshake. Even with four fingers missing, Dad's thumb firmly clamped my right hand against the paw that was his palm. As he settled behind the steering wheel and started the engine, I repeated a promise to write. I stepped away and watched the pale-blue sedan stir the dust as it slowly crunched forward over the gravel until the first curve took it from view. I turned and marched forward into my new life.

Fitting In

Like arriving at Seattle Prep or turning out for football, I wanted to fit into the unknown routine without getting embarrassed. I listened carefully to whatever my guardian angel said. For the first eight days I'd be a "postulant," a Latin derivative referring to a person asking for something; I was asking the

Order to accept me. Brother Ellis explained that all postulants would wear casual laymen's clothes—denims or khaki pants and sport shirts—until officially accepted as novices. Then we'd be issued cassocks.

I began to pick up the Jesuit language:

* "Novice Master," a term with a plantation ring stood as the official title for Father Elliott. He was the saintly man appointed to guide novices of the Oregon Province into the spiritual life of a Jesuit.

* The "Oregon Province" drew almost all its novices from the states it covered: Oregon, Washington, Idaho, Montana, and Alaska.

* "Beadle," a term from the Middle Ages for the student who assisted an instructor in a university. In the Novitiate, this was the second-year novice Father Elliott selected to handle routine tasks like assigning work duties for the month, such as who would wait tables, wash dishes, or polish chapel floors.

* "Recreation times" referred to times when talking was permitted: the thirty to forty minutes after the midday meal and after supper, the ninety-minute afternoon break when we were allowed to sign up for exercise activities outdoors like basketball, handball, walking, or working in the gardens.

* "Juniors" were Jesuits, about fifty strong, in their third and fourth year in the Order who were segregated in the north side of the building. At the end of the two-year novitiate they became official Jesuits by taking the "first vows" of poverty, chastity, and obedience ("final vows" would come more than a decade later after ordination to the priesthood). Juniors studied full-time. I recognized a few who had been two years ahead of me

at Prep. Brother Ellis told me novices could not speak to juniors even if we passed within a few feet of each other when they were coming off the basketball court and we were going on. The oddness of reacting to them like invisible people wore off quickly because "that was the rule." I conscientiously fell into step with the rules.

✤ "Magnum Silentium" was the solemn silence that settled over the entire building from 9:30 p.m. until a clanging bell woke us at 5:00 a.m.

The second-year novices had time on their hands because they had finished summer school before our arrival. Together we awaited the second wave of postulants to arrive on September 7th. Brother Ellis let me know the daily routine we enjoyed was less demanding than the routine that would come in September.

Each day, Father Elliott delivered to us postulants lectures on the Order and its rules. My ignorance of the Jesuits probably was close to that of a Marine recruit who doesn't have a clue what *Semper Fidelis* stands for before he goes to boot camp and puts on the uniform. Although I had been around Jesuits at Prep for almost four years, I didn't know what they did when they went to their living quarters—how much they prayed, when they attended Mass, how often they went to Confession.

I began to learn from the novice master Jesuit history. The life of Ignatius Loyola, the Spanish founder of the Jesuits, followed the plot line of a fast-paced novel: soldier at eighteen, captive of the French following the Battle of Pamplona where a cannonball shattered his leg, an ex-military man following his recuperation, spiritual convert, soul-searching ascetic in a cave near Manresa in Catalonia, developer of the "Spiritual Exercises."

During the last half of August, Father Elliott began infusing the rules of the Order like a physician overseeing an intravenous feeding, one Ignatius Loyola had bottled with the spiritual discipline four hundred years before. I had no idea I was about to inadvertently set up the novice master for our introduction to an important Ignatian rule.

The warmth of summer allowed recreation times to take place outdoors, near the south wing of the building. The sunny weather and my sense of being on the right path in life energized me. I joked. I laughed. I'd punctuate my exchanges with a slap on the back, a friendly elbow, or a playful punch. The novices took my kidding and horseplay in stride. On the third day, a novice who had graduated from Prep the previous year was standing relaxed and unprepared for my playful shove. He stumbled backward before falling on the grass. I quickly offered my hand and apologized while helping him to his feet. Both novices and postulants smiled and chuckled.

The next morning, we postulants filed into the lecture classroom and took our places. The bone-white walls and deep-brown long tables we sat at set a solemn tone. We faced Father Elliott, who sat erect behind a small, bare desk elevated on a six-inch dais.

He introduced the Order's Rule 32: *Regula de tactu vitando* (Rule regarding the avoidance of touch). Though not named, I soon learned my pushes, shoves, and even slight touches on the shoulder had been violating this rule. A semaphore blush swept over me. *Why hadn't my guardian angel told me I was breaking a rule? Was it bad form for him to preempt the novice master's exposition of the rules?*

I did wonder why our basketball games didn't violate the rule of touch when we'd elbow our way into position under the hoop and didn't hold back the push for advantage. Not all touches were considered the same; some could be overlooked.

There was no discussion or allusion linking the rule of touch to the risk of homosexuality. Given my naiveté, it never crossed my mind. There was, however, a prohibition against "particular friendships" (another term I added to my Jesuit lexicon), which I came to understand meant preferred friends like those I had in high school. The ideal Jesuit friendship emerged as equidistant from all brothers. I could understand this as an ideal, but wondered whether it was humanly possible.

My unwitting violation of Rule 32 sensitized me to the steady influx of the Jesuit code of conduct. I was certain there were subtler rules I would come to know, just as a young boy I had learned to read, with the help of a candle, secret messages written with lemon juice.

After eight days, donning a cassock transformed me from postulant to novice, who could sign my name, "James Tracy, N.S.J." (Novice of the Society of Jesus). I wondered whether I was a rookie putting on a professional uniform at tryouts, there to see if I could measure up and really make the team.

I looked forward to soaking up the spirit, zeal, and virtues of the Jesuits. I recalled the Catechism question imprinted at St. Catherine's—"Why did God make you?"—and knew Jesuit training would add horsepower to its answer, "to know Him, to love Him, and to serve Him in this world, and to be happy with Him forever in the next." The "in the next" subtly emphasized my pursuit of God.

With the arrival of the second wave of postulants in September, our entry class swelled to thirty-two. As we in the first wave had done, they learned where to put dirty laundry, that meals were eaten in silence except for asking for food in Latin, and how to dampen their impatience to wear cassocks. I watched to see how many touched in jest. A few did. Learning Rule 32 stopped that.

With our first-year class at full strength, Father Elliott's morning talks schooled us in the twice-a-day meditations, one hour in the morning and thirty minutes in the afternoon. I learned how to imagine a scene from the New Testament, like the Sermon on the Mount. I'd see Jesus facing a crowd and hear him say the words I read in St. Matthew's gospel, which was open before me. Of course, the image dimmed when the discomfort of kneeling on the wood slat of the prie-dieu broke my concentration. I did my best to refocus on the scene. I struggled with, "Blessed are the poor in spirit." *Who are the "poor in spirit"?* Aching knees and guessing at the meaning of scripture undermined meditation, a practice I knew could only get better.

PICKING ITALIAN PRUNE PLUMS

In mid-September, we novices became the primary work force to pick the ripened plums hanging heavy in the orchard. The harvesting had to be completed within a five-to-eight-day window. The work suspended our Latin class, lectures on the rules, and mid-day recreation breaks.

The Order relied primarily on donations to support the Novitiate, but the Sheridan Jesuits took every opportunity to lower expenses and to generate income. The deep-purple Italian prune plums that ripened on the property were harvested each September, sold to Del Monte Foods, and stood as the community's biggest money-maker.

Early on the picking day, experienced second-year novices moved into a target section of the orchard. They advanced from tree to tree with long wooden poles topped with grappling hooks to shake the plums free, but not too vigorously. We arrived after breakfast chores, picked up galvanized buckets, and invaded our assigned area. There we fell on our knees (something we were getting used to) and began picking up the fallen fruit. We emptied our full buckets into boxes between the rows of trees. Every hour novices carried full boxes to the edge of the road for pickup. Talking was permitted, with the understanding that our mission was harvesting plums.

Yellow jacket wasps feed on fruit, especially plums split open by hitting the ground. After one sting, I mastered the art of picking up an opened plum without stopping a yellow jacket's exit. Occasionally I heard a "Dammit!" that signaled a sting. Spiritual training had not yet purified a novice's vocabulary.

Even Father Elliott came during the early afternoon and worked beside us for a couple of hours. His presence was edifying. However, after he left, mid-afternoon fatigue opened the door to horseplay. A few brothers began testing the accuracy of their throws of mushy plums at unsuspecting fellow novices. The key was to make a throw from a distance that wouldn't give away the thrower—about as far as a catcher would fire a baseball to throw out a runner trying to steal second base. My few throws weren't accurate. Only once did I get hit by return fire. This horsing around lightened the seriousness of my new life.

The day ended with us loading the filled boxes on the two-ton Army truck that inched along the road. Three second-year novices manned the truck: one to drive and two to help load and later unload at the Del Monte plant in Salem, thirty miles away.

As we trudged the half-mile up the gravel road to the Novitiate, I wondered how much the banter, plum-throwing, laughter, and fatigue matched my brother's experience when he joined his fraternity at the U of W. I recalled Ron describing the sadistic initiation that included freshman pledges being forced to eat food they disliked to the point of vomiting into buckets placed on the dining table. Later his fraternity added the upside of pushing him and other freshmen to get good grades and to compete in sports against other fraternities, where he did well in golf.

I hadn't yet experienced anything like being forced to eat food I disliked. I enjoyed the growing camaraderie of working together with my fellow novices toward a common goal. At his first lecture after the end of the harvest, Father Elliott announced that we had harvested the largest crop to date, over forty tons. Of course, he didn't disclose how much income the plums had generated. Bragging rights were improper, because we knew that pride was one of the seven deadly sins.

THE SPIRITUAL EXERCISES

Early in October, we freshly-minted novices streamed from our cubicles into the dimly lit corridor and again headed to the evening lecture. Two-foot rosaries, unique to novices, dangled from our cincture belts and jingled as we moved along. They fell silent only after we found our places. Father Elliott walked in last, a thin manila folder in hand, to take his routine seat—front, center, and elevated. He scanned our upturned faces as his hand found well-worn notes. His voice, which always lacked the resonance of a pulpit preacher, nevertheless clearly found every corner of the room.

I settled into my chair like a first-time roller-coaster rider not knowing what to expect. In a measured, solemn, maestro-manner, Father Elliot began describing the long retreat that would begin the next morning. He outlined the basic rules for the next thirty days. He said the nightly *magnum silentium* would expand to all our waking hours with two brief breaks part-way through the thirty days. Silence for long periods was as unknown to me as climbing Mt. Everest. I wondered how I would suppress the urge to talk. The long retreat was shaping up as a one-way talk. The novice master, St. Ignatius, and God would talk; we would listen.

Next, he briefed us on a key Ignatian exercise. "The particular *examen* is an examination of conscience carried out twice a day, the first time around noon, and the second in the evening. They help root out sins and shortcomings."

He went on to describe how important it was to be aware of how often we fail God and ourselves in the hours between each *examen*. He encouraged us to tally our failures in a small notebook. He ended with, "These particular *examens,* beginning in this long retreat, are to continue each day for the rest of your Jesuit life."

I was sure I wouldn't be committing mortal sins, but I wondered whether my interrupting a person in a conversation qualified as a venial sin. Certainly it's rude and a fault. Is my reflexive unbelieving "What?" to a dumb statement a sin? Even if it doesn't qualify as a sin to be confessed, it's a shortcoming I would still need to root out. I zealously took up the tool of the particular *examen.*

The next morning, Father Elliott again spoke to us first-year novices. He placed his hand on a small, worn, leather book he'd put on the desk when he had first sat down. He began where he had left off the evening before, "As you came in this morning, each of you received a copy of *The Spiritual Exercises* of St. Ignatius. The wisdom and instructions in these Exercises never become outdated. You will begin to understand and appreciate them in this first retreat, an understanding and appreciation that will deepen as you revisit them during your annual eight-day retreats in the years to come."

Over time, I would come to believe that the repetition of retreats was like the re-inking of *Semper Fidelis* tattoos on those Marines whose loyalty to the Corps never fades.

Father Elliott continued. "You will see in the table of contents that these Exercises are divided into four weeks. But these are not the seven-day weeks you are used to. The work of the first week will take more than seven days, while the fourth week will take fewer."

I came to view the first week as a metaphor for the first weeks of basic military training that toughens raw recruits. Father Elliott pointed out that we were embarking on what Ignatius had done in the cave at Manresa. There the Jesuit founder dwelt on his sinfulness, took on the yoke of penance, and meditated. During this first week we were going to follow the founder's lead.

Rather than defending myself in a fight against the blows of a strong opponent, I was to be the aggressor against myself. Ignatius, in the guise of the novice master, was talking directly to me. He was coaching me in hard-scraping self-examinations intended to flay away the skin of pride and to search for sins and faults in thought, word, and deed, which I must grieve over and remove. I accepted the job as part of the Jesuit boot camp to toughen me for the battles ahead as a "soldier of Christ," a phrase Ignatius echoed from St. Paul.

Ignatius set the stage for the Spiritual Exercises in writing, "The purpose of these Exercises is to help the exercitant to conquer himself, and to regulate his life so that he will not be influenced in his decisions by any inordinate attachment." He followed that opening with the refrain I had known since the first grade at St. Catherine's and that had become my strongest belief over the twelve years since then: "Man is created to praise, reverence, and serve God our Lord, and by this means to save his soul." I knew my sexual sins in high school made me fall short of this belief. Now the Exercises would help me get up and get going.

Ignatius aimed this first week of the long retreat at fostering proper desires: "I shall here beg for an ever increasing and intense sorrow and tears for my sins." Father Elliott began schooling us in Ignatian meditation that blended imagination, reasoning, and will.

Ignatius writes in the first exercise, devoted to sins, "the mental image will consist of imagining, and considering my soul imprisoned in its corruptible body, and my entire being in this vale of tears as an exile among brute beasts." He goes on, "I shall ask for pain, tears, and suffering with Christ suffering. In the present meditation I shall ask for shame and confusion, for I see how many souls have been damned for a single mortal sin, and how often I have deserved to be damned eternally for the many sins I have committed."

I felt the guilt and sinful weight of French kissing and heavy petting that I'd done in high school. Ignatius kept pressing forward in reminding me that I had sinned many more times than the first sinners, angels who "fell from grace into sin and were cast from heaven into hell" as devils. The searchlight of self-examination showed my sins as more grievous than the sins of angels, the sin of Adam and Eve, and the sin of people condemned to hell for a single sin. The exercises of the first week demanded that I submerge myself in self-loathing, from which only Christ could save me. And submerge I did, plunging myself in regret and the acid of self-criticism.

The daily meditations of the first week drummed home how sorry I should be for my sins. I experienced a deepening sense of worthlessness, which the later parts of the Exercise were supposed to address. But we were not to think ahead to Christ's saving actions. Anticipating the urge to escape self-degradation, Ignatius had penned the following resolution for us to make our own: "I will not think of pleasant and joyful things as heaven, the Resurrection, etc., for such consideration of joy and delight will hinder the feeling of sin, sorrow, and tears I should have for my sins."

In addition, Ignatius advocated three forms of exterior penance: regarding food, sleeping, and chastising the flesh. This last form he elaborated: "This is done by wearing hair shirts, cords, or iron chains on the body, or by scourging or wounding oneself, or by other kinds of austerities."

Apparently to avoid extremes, Ignatius added a bit of prudence in appending the following: "What seems the most suitable and safest thing in doing penance is for the pain to be felt in the flesh, without penetration to the bones, thus causing pain but not illness. Therefore it seems more fitting to scourge oneself with light cords, which cause exterior pain, than in another way that might cause internal infirmity."

In the middle of that first week of the Exercises, we were issued our personal instruments of penance: a whip, the *flagellum*, and two penance chains, the *catenulae*, one for an arm and the other for a leg. The "flag" (pronounced with a short "a" and a soft "g"), stretched out, was about 18-inches long. It was made of sturdy white cord braided into a thumb-thick short handle that felt solid when held in a tight grip. Several stiff knotted strands of cord blossomed out of the handle. Lying loose on my bed, the flag looked innocuous. But when I was bare to the waist with left hand on my head and my right hand and arm was swinging it hard several times across my back, it delivered a good deal of pain. The *flagellatio* (applying the flag to the back) wasn't a blood-spattering exercise, although a few times I noticed afterwards few red sprinkles on my T-shirt. This exercise never reached the pain I experienced in high school when putting undersized football shoes on feet already adorned with broken blisters. Both, however, shared the imperative of, "You need to pay a price for what you are striving for."

I learned that the Sisters of the Precious Blood, a cloistered order of nuns, made the *flagella* in their convent not far away in Portland. "Precious blood" juxtaposed with the whips seemed fitting. Mom later told me that when we lived in Portland, she had helped these nuns by running errands they were not allowed to do because they were sheltered from the outside world. I never told Mom what penitential products they manufactured.

I found the chains more difficult than the *flag* for two reasons. The first was that the Jesuit novices made the *catenulae*, sometimes carelessly, for the next year's class. *Catenulae*-making converted wire, about the diameter of angel hair pasta, into prickly links joined and shaped into bands like a blood pressure cuff—one band for an arm and one for a thigh, both cinched tight against the skin. The manufacturing novice was often lax in filing off the jagged tips left after cutting the wire. His laxity left sharp edges which engraved biceps and thighs with scratches and minor cuts.

The second reason the chains were more challenging was they needled the skin for the better part of two hours, while the *flag* was over and done in a short time. But I'd be exaggerating to say these penitential rituals were terrible. They fit hand-in-glove as reminders of sinfulness and simply became a routine part of our life. The beadle would put up a *catenulae* or *flagellatio* sign on the bulletin board several times a month indicating which one was the penance *du jour.*

Nearing the end of the first week, I, the pummeled sinner, felt like a boxer after twelve rounds, with arms hanging limp by my side. At this point, Father Elliott introduced *Rules for the Discernment of Spirits,* one of the four sets of rules in the Spiritual Exercises. These "discernment" rules outlined scenarios where the "evil spirit" and the "good spirit" fight over me through the uses of "consolation" and "desolation." The

rules were supposed to school us on how to tell the difference
between the spirits, and how the evil spirit could use the love
of our Creator and Lord to lead us away from Him. Ignatius's
sketch of the seesaw battle for my soul never struck me as a
metaphor. The Spiritual Exercises portrayed the struggle over
my soul as a real war between genuine spirits. These rules were
to be the truth-detectors for knowing whether positive feelings
were a camouflaged trap from the devil or a depression was a
test from God. I felt at a loss on how to sort them out. However,
my confusion didn't stop me from soldiering on with complete
confidence that God, St. Ignatius, and Father Elliott knew what
they were doing.

Even though Father Elliott skipped the other three sets of
rules, I read them. In the final set, *Rules for Thinking with the
Church*, St. Ignatius wrote, "1. Putting aside all private judgment, we should keep our minds prepared and ready to obey
promptly and in all things the true spouse of Christ our Lord,
our Holy Mother, the hierarchical Church." And Rule 13 followed with: "If we wish to be sure that we are right in all things,
we should always be ready to accept this principle: I will believe
that the white I see is black, if the hierarchical Church so defines it." I sailed by the rule without questioning, without noticing really, and without recalling my high school exchanges
with Father Menard about the Church's punishment of Galileo.
Looking back, I believe my fervor must have reflexively quarantined the rule and cut off any serious reflection.

With the afternoon recreation of basketball or handball on
hold during the Exercises, I took up solitary walks. I often sought
out the abandoned apple orchard west of the main building,
where few people went. There I sometimes found a doe and her
fawn feasting on fallen unclaimed fruit. I'd stop about twenty
feet away from them. Then we'd begin our standoff. I admired
her milk-chocolate pelt that glistened on drizzling days. While

keeping an eye on me, she'd mosey to a further tree, taking her speckled offspring with her. I wondered what she made of this two-legged intruder who interrupted her mid-afternoon meal.

These walks, especially ones in the rain, brought back memories of sloshing through my paper route while privately rehearsing Catechism answers. Now I had heard the "know, love, and serve God" of the Baltimore Catechism repeated in the Ignatian military cadence of, "I came from God; I belong to God; I am destined for God." The connection between my first Catechism and the Spiritual Exercises snapped together perfectly.

The second, third, and fourth weeks of the long retreat failed to shine through the dark clouds of that first week. While Ignatius built the latter weeks around Christ's public life, His suffering and crucifixion to atone for my sins, and His resurrection, they didn't lift me out of the pit of the first week. That first week had confirmed my sinfulness, which had partly fueled my entrance into the Order, and still stalked me.

Like a swimmer submerged too long, I broke the retreat's surface of silence and gulped the fresh air of our limited talking. I emerged thankful that the thirty days were done, although I was better acquainted with the solace of silence. I knew my primary work was building a spiritual life, a life focused on meditation, particular *examens*, spiritual reading, and mastering the rules and spirit of the Order.

One odd event had occurred during the long retreat. In October, part-way through the Exercises, Father Elliott had broken the rhythm of an evening lecture in saying, "Brothers, I encourage you to pray for the resolution of a world situation." I assumed the vagueness was to avoid distracting us from our spiritual work. I thought perhaps the Cold War with Russia might have escalated to the brink of real war. Only months later did I learn what had happened: the new military leader of

Egypt, Gamal Abdel Nasser, had nationalized the Suez Canal, an action that led Israel, with the aid of England and France, to invade Egypt. Father Elliott's vague allusion to the outside world underlined how isolated we novices were.

At the end of the retreat, the beadle distributed letters held back while we were trying to relive the days St. Ignatius spent in the cave outside Manresa. Having told my folks that I wouldn't be given letters during the retreat, I eagerly read the single letter that had arrived. The handwriting told me it was from Mom. She wrote, "Grandma died of a heart attack on October 12th." She went on to write, "The doctor had come to the house earlier in the day and examined Ma. The doctor didn't find anything life-threatening or requiring hospitalization. She had been watching TV with me, your father, and Ron. She said she was tired and was going to bed early. I went to check on her about a half hour later. When I went into her room and saw her face, I knew she was dead. I went back into the living room and said, 'I think Ma has died.' Ron said, 'No, Mom, I'll go and get a pulse.' He came back in just a few minutes and said, 'I couldn't get a pulse. I think she's gone. We need to call the doctor.'"

Mom added that she had called the Novitiate and had spoken to Father Elliott. "He said that even if you weren't in the long retreat, you wouldn't be allowed to come home because the Order doesn't consider the death of a grandmother a death within the 'immediate family,' the only reason a novice would be allowed to leave the Novitiate to attend a funeral."

I took a deep breath, felt tears rim my eyes. I left my cubicle and went to the chapel where I said a prayer for Grandma. *She had been a part of my life since I was six. She and Mom took care of me in the early days of rheumatic fever. After Mom went to work, Grandma took care of me when I got sick and had to stay home from school; she fixed lunches for me when I walked home at noon time. How can anyone say she wasn't a member of my immediate family?* But knowing

Mom, I figured she probably was too sad to plead the case for my coming home for Grandma's funeral.

I left the chapel and went back to my cubicle to change clothes for afternoon recreation. I didn't tell any of my brothers about Grandma's death. I just wanted to grieve by myself without the interruption of condolences.

ROUTINES

November started a post-retreat routine of a single class in Latin (our first and only first-semester college course), a lecture by Father Elliott, and our first fifteen-minute examination of conscience before lunch. The twice-a-day examination of conscience served as a sluice box in which I searched for sins and shortcomings that needed to be expunged from my character. Having just emerged from the long retreat with its drumbeat of personal sinfulness, it took me awhile to notice that opportunities for sin were few and far between. Yet the microscope of these daily self-examinations magnified a critical thought, a flippant remark, or an unnecessary word during a time of silence. Any shortcoming or infraction justified self-criticism and remorse.

Outside of retreats, morning meditations were largely self-directed. Gospel episodes of Christ's life, beginning with his birth, became meditation stops for a good part of the year. After Christmas, meditation pivoted to Christ's public life of preaching, by which he had become popular with rank-and-file Jews. I believed his popularity, accelerated with miracles like raising people from the dead, could understandably rub the professional clergy the wrong way. I did my best meditating each morning and afternoon, blending one part Gospel with two parts imagination. Morning mediation, with its 5:30 a.m. start, was the most challenging.

Sleep, even when kneeling, released the balloons of imagery. A loud slap-bang sometimes snapped me awake after the New Testament had slipped out of my sleep-slackened hand and hit the floor. Sometimes a snore from the cubicle next door would prod me to start my own sleep-evasion tactics. I tried biting my tongue, rotating between kneeling and standing, and opening the window opposite my cubicle to the chilly wind. My brothers and I never discussed our methods for fighting sleep, and I don't recall Father Elliott prescribing specific remedies either.

While fighting my battle with sleep, I was sometimes stymied to find topics for meditation. The first Christmas at Sheridan I enjoyed the smell of evergreen boughs piled inside the ten-by-fifteen-foot crèche assembled inside the chapel's Communion rail. There, incarnated in plaster, the shepherds, wise men, animals, Joseph, and Mary stood or knelt around the mangered infant Jesus. During meditation, though, I felt awkward, silly really, trying to carry on a prayerful dialogue with an infant. Imagining a newborn with a fully developed divine mind that was attuned to my prayer just didn't make sense.

Bright Spot

"Villa day" was a mid-week break from the Novitiate's stiff daily routine. Wearing our grungiest clothes, we trudged the mile to the twenty-by-forty-foot one-room retreat in the woods. The building stood amid tall Douglas firs. Scavenged pane windows punctuated the graying clapboard sides. The interior had just a few support beams, which I'm sure met no county code. But I'm also sure no county inspector knew the villa existed. With no running water, electricity, or toilet, the only amenity was a hundred-gallon drum fashioned into a pot-bellied heater we stuffed with wood we had split. At rough-hewn, picnic-size tables, we ate off Army-surplus metal platters filled with hot food ladled from Army-surplus containers the Army-surplus truck carried slowly from the Novitiate's kitchen over the rutted road to this villa refuge. When rain kept most of us inside for the afternoon, we played monopoly, cards, or chess, all laced with the din of laughter and banter. Villa days became sunshine in the rainy season. They knotted tighter the bonds among the more than fifty of us novices.

I marvel at the unspoken way in which old relationships shifted and new ones webbed together. With Frank, one of my closest friends at Prep, I shared the most background. We had played varsity football together, double-dated together, and entered the Order together. His ready smile, dry wit, and low-key laugh made him easy to like and want as a friend. Now, as Jesuit novices, we had recalibrated our relationship to one that was not as familiar as the one we had before. It was still friendly, but a tad more reserved. I'd describe it as "more respectful." For my part, I felt it was a retreaded friendship, one closer to those I was building with other novices.

The Villa
(Jesuit Oregon Province Archives)

Brother Marsh, a Montana native, entered the Order after completing one year at Gonzaga University. His grin was so big it almost squeezed his eyes shut behind the glasses that often slipped down his nose. I first got to know him on the basketball court, where he released a deadly jump shot before I could raise my hand to block it.

He quickly earned a reputation for wanting to discuss "deep" topics like a philosophical point he'd come across in the heavy spiritual reading like Dietrich Von Hildebrands's *The Transformation in Christ*. Discussions in the Novitiate, however, were mostly limited to "recreation" time (the thirty or forty minutes of relaxing time) after completing the chores that followed meals. We were not routinely free to choose with whom to recreate. Rather, we were reshuffled and assigned to a group of two to four brothers. Besides making sure we mixed with everyone over time, I'm also sure such assignments aimed at preventing cliques or particular friendships from forming.

On the occasions when we were free to choose who to chat with, many of our brothers passed over Brother Marsh because they didn't want to spend thirty to forty minutes discussing "deep topics" with him. I did. He usually led our chat into the book he was reading. Much of the time I felt I was running behind him and trying to keep pace. Although I was behind him, I never got lost. Our conversations nurtured the "whys" and "why nots" that I came to sense we shared.

SHIFTING GEARS

Forging ahead into a new semester felt like mastering the manual gear shift of my brother's '35 Ford—pushing up and pulling down the stick through the gears. College classes increased to three: Latin Prose, English Precepts, and Intermediate Greek. The last was a surprise, because I'd not taken Greek in high school and only later learned that who-ever assigned classes assumed I had. I accepted the placement without mentioning my worry about keeping up. The reflex-ive thought, "It must be God's will," helped me.

I decided that my assignment to the Greek class was an ex-ample that fit well with Father Elliott's talk on Jesuit discipline encapsulated in the pithy Latin sentence, *Age quod agis* (Do what you're doing.). I took up the phrase as if it were a ban-ner I could carry into unwelcome tasks, like being assigned to Greek class or to walk with a companion who talked a lot and rarely listened. *Age quod agis* sanded smooth the edges of frus-tration and soothed me with a sense of doing God's will. In the case of the Greek class, my conformity to God's will earned my first C in the Order, a fact I didn't learn until years later because we were not allowed to see our transcripts or know our grades. My hunch is the Order wanted to protect those with good grades from the sin of pride and those with low grades from discouragement.

In January, along with others, I was scanning the bulle-tin board outside the beadle's room. Because talking wasn't permitted, no one commented on the postings. We'd quietly work our way forward to read the latest assignments neatly typed on three-by-five cards. My eyes fell on, *Frater Tracy est no-vus tonsor.* I'd been appointed the new barber. The announce-ment, really a command, in a small way mirrored the Jesuit ideal of blind obedience, which dictates that if the pope were to order a Jesuit to serve the Church in a distant country, the Jesuit must leave immediately without asking for the means to get there.

Now, as one of two barbers for the fifty-plus Novices, my work assignment after the noon and evening meals shifted from kitchen chores or buffing floors to buzzing crew cuts and keeping parted hair short and neat. The outgoing barber told me to show up after lunch at the barbershop, an alcove in a small second-floor classroom, where in two sessions he'd school me in the art of barbering.

"You hold the comb on a slight angle like this," he began as he held the eight-inch black comb at a 45-degree slope. "With the comb in your left hand, you move it around the head starting at the low hair line. Use the clippers to cut off the hair sticking through the teeth of the comb."

The novice in the chair cleared his throat while his behind searched for a more comfortable spot on the aging barber chair.

My trainer continued, "Keep the angle of the comb steady to avoid putting stair-steps up the side of the head."

And that's how my tutorial in barbering started. It ended, as he had said, after two days of oversight. With a friendly smile he offered a sage comment, "Remember, Brother Tracy, because hair grows, the only difference between a bad haircut and a good haircut is one week."

I soon learned that the novices who wore crew cuts preferred a level square flattop. My first dozen attempts failed to get the upright hair parallel to the horizon. This left any brother unlucky enough to end up in my chair with the need to carry his head slightly tilted or to accept his lopsided appearance as God's will.

Within a few months I'd begun to master the art of sculpting heads. I also began to overrate my barbering skills. Brother Harrison stood over six-feet-six-inches tall. In fact, he'd played center on the Santa Clara University basketball team before entering the Order. For a tall man he had the unusual habit of maintaining very erect posture; he never walked with self-conscious rounded shoulders or a bent head as many extra-tall men do to avoid hitting low overhangs. He stood out. His jet black hair contrasted sharply with his alabaster skin.

While putting the final trim at the back of his head, I glanced down at the comb my fellow barber had dropped on the floor. Then I heard the growl of the electric clippers, the sound that comes when mowing especially thick hair. My breath braked to a stop as I glanced back at the two-inch square of white scalp staring at me. "Uh, oh," escaped my lips. With no way of repairing the damage short of applying black shoe polish, I quietly apologized. Brother Harrison continued to walk erect, advertising the limits of my barbering skills.

Of course, the humor of my mistake didn't escape the notice of my brothers. In fact, humor became yeast that lightened the heavy atmosphere of the Novitiate. In February of 1957, each first-year novice was measured for a new cassock, a companion for the used one we had been issued for everyday use. Because the Order was committed to a life of poverty, the cassock measurements were forwarded to a manufacturer in Formosa. Reasonably priced new cassocks returned in time for Easter. In donning our newly minted black robes I and others commented on the noticeable pleats around the shoulders and the extra fabric between the waist and ankles. Obviously, a dress factory with little or no experience in making cassocks for the Catholic clergy had done the job. We began trading quips like, "Where's the parasol?" and "I dreamt I was ordained in my new Maidenform-osa cassock."

In the midst of our chuckling over our new cassocks, I was struck by the wry smile on Brother Dahlquist's face. He was a couple of years older than me, very quiet, and had a left arm slowed by polio. He was easy to overlook in the midst of bantering and quick wit. He never was the first to speak in a conversation, and when he did, he spoke slowly. I recognized his slow speech did not reflect a dull mind. When I remained quiet, his wit emerged like a rabbit from its warren. I looked forward to his company when assigned to the same recreation group.

THE CHARITY BALL

In mid-February, Father Elliott introduced the *Exercitium Caritatis* (Exercise of Charity). He explained that the following Wednesday evening after recreation, all novices would assemble in the lecture room. There he would call three first-year novices, one at a time, to kneel on the dais in front of him. He then would call out the name of another novice to start the Exercise of Charity. The job of the called-upon novice was to state a shortcoming in the behavior of the kneeling novice. Father Elliott would then continue to call out the names of other novices until he felt it was time to move on to the second and then on to the evening's final recipient of the Exercise of Charity. This exercise would continue once-a-week until each first-year novice had run the gauntlet of what the second-year novices called the "Charity Ball."

As I walked into the lecture room that evening, the suspense of not knowing who would be called hung in the air. I felt more anxious than I did in high school when I knew I might be called on to recite a poem in class or when I approached the microphone to address the student body. I calculated the odds of being called that first night as one in ten. Those odds didn't take my foot off the accelerator ramping up my heartbeat. Because we weren't assigned seating, I found a chair in the second-to-last row of desks, definitely not in the last row, which could signal my anxiety, nor in the first row, which would put my face in close range of Father Elliott's gaze.

I inhaled deeply until Father Elliott called out the first name, "Brother Henriot." He was a bespectacled redhead who had entered the Order after attending Santa Clara for two years. His manner was consistently pleasant and marked by the ability to spark conversations with an energy that likely came from his experience as a high school and college debater. I couldn't think of any way to criticize him even with my recently honed skills of self-criticism. My discomfort eased as five other brothers gave bland and quickly forgotten comments about his actions and personality. The beadle, following Father Elliott's directive, wrote down all comments. The next day Father Elliot would review the notes one-on-one with the individual novice.

As Brother Henriot was retaking his seat, I heard, "Brother Tracy." My breathing halted as I absorbed the name. It seemed a long time passed before I rose. I sidestepped between the brothers sitting to my right and made my way to the dais where I knelt before Father Elliott.

"Brother Steiner," he called out.

"It seems to me that Brother Tracy is too often sarcastic in his conversations."

"Brother Grant."

"Brother Tracy can be sharp in his comments."

"Brother Scordan."

"Brother Tracy is quick to make jokes that sometimes can hurt people's feelings."

"Brother Peterson."

"Brother Tracy sometimes jumps in quickly with words that cut people off."

I don't recall how many fellow novices Father Elliott called on, maybe eight. But by comment number three the theme was clear.

When Father Elliott released me from the hazing, I focused on the polished tips of my shoes as I walked back to my place. I wobbled mentally, but not in my gait. I don't recall who was called next. My breath was shallow after my dance at the Charity Ball.

The next afternoon, Brother Schmidt, the beadle, came to my cubicle where I was half-heartedly studying Latin and still licking my wounds from the night before. "*Frater Tracy, Pater Elliott vult videre te.*" The invitation to see the novice master didn't make me look forward to it. My leaden legs carried me out of the cubicle row and down the hall thirty feet to the darkly varnished door of Father Elliott's rooms. My knock evoked a muffled distant, "Come in." As I stepped through the door I was startled not to find the novice master sitting behind his desk where he had always been the few times I'd seen him before one-on-one. He stepped back into his office from the small adjacent bedroom, which seemed more like a large closet from what I could see. That private place also warehoused the spiritual books that he had dispensed during previous visits.

As he seated himself in the chair behind the desk, he pointed to the chair across from him. His hand motion was liquid like a symphony director's but without a hint of ordering or harshness.

As I sat down, he glanced at the notes the beadle had left and then slid them aside.

"What did you hear last evening?" he asked.

"Well, I certainly heard I'm sharp-tongued and more insensitive than I thought I was."

"Yes, they did talk about your comments and conversation. Was there anything else you heard?"

"I kept hearing the same thing said several times but in different ways. I really didn't hear much else."

"They did repeat themselves, but it does give you something to work on."

"It certainly does."

He acknowledged my taking more hits than the others, and added, "While it's something to work on, don't brood too much about the comments, and don't let hurt feelings distract you from the spiritual path."

He then moved on to other topics like how far I had read in Rodriquez's *Life of the Saints*. His leaving my obvious major flaw so abruptly and matter-of-factly was soothing. I felt Father

Elliott applying compresses to my bruised ego and sensed a fatherly comfort.

THE UNEXPECTED

During a spring evening after recreation, another first-year novice came out of breath to my cubicle. "You have a telephone call downstairs in the visitors' parlor," he said.

I rose and hurried down to the first floor, where I found the phone receiver lying next to its cradle.

"Hello," I said.

"Jim, is that you?"

"Yes," I said while searching for recognition.

It was a young woman's voice. I could hear indistinct background voices. My memory whirred.

"How are you?" she said.

Her total seven words spun like the fruits and bells on a slot machine until they stopped on "Phyllis," a girl I'd dated six or seven times after the breakup with Maureen.

"Phyllis?"

An acknowledging laugh was followed by, "What are you doing tonight?"

The disjointed syllables of those last words let me know she'd been drinking.

"I'm...," I scrambled for what to say.

"Are you coming back?" she said. More background noise.... Then "click."

I put the receiver back in its cradle, turned, and retraced my steps up the stairs to my cubicle and desk. I was puzzled. I certainly didn't feel any magnetic pull toward dating or life on a college campus. That night I dropped into sleep as I usually did, within five minutes.

Before Latin class the next morning, the beadle told me the Novice Master wanted to see me.

"I understand you were called to the phone last night," Father Elliott began.

"Yes, Father."

"Tell me about it."

"A brother came to my cubicle and said I had a phone call, so I went down and answered it."

"Did he tell you who was calling?"

"No, he just said I had a call."

"And...?"

"When I picked up the phone, it took me a minute to recognize who it was."

"And...?"

"It was a girl I dated briefly in high school."

"How long did you talk?"

"Less than a minute."

"How did it end?"

"I think she hung up."

"Did you have any idea she was going to call?"

"No, not at all."

Father Elliot paused and looked at his hands, clasped loosely together and resting on the desk before him.

Looking up at me, he began to speak calmly, "I regret that the brother came and got you. As you know, phone calls are not allowed, but it doesn't sound like you were responsible for the call." His initial interrogator tone had evaporated.

"Have you thought much about the call?"

"Not much at all."

"We never know when we will be taken off guard, because we can't predict events in our lives. Let me know if anything like this happens again or if you find yourself dwelling on the call."

With my "Yes, Father," I was dismissed.

I thought Father Elliott took me at my word. I never spoke about the call to any of my brothers, not even to my Prep brothers who had known Phyllis. I pulled the covers over the incident with the consoling thought of how much better I felt this year than last year when I was heavily involved with Maureen. I had chosen a spiritual path and wasn't tormented by any sexual sinning.

In 1957, Easter Sunday fell on April 21st and reminded me that by this time the year before I was close to applying to the Order. Now I felt the rhythm of Novitiate life as vividly as I had felt the throb of the '53 Ford I'd left behind with my brother. I felt comfortable in Latin and Greek classes. I kept plugging away at meditation. Summer was fast approaching.

NOVITIATE—YEAR 2

August brought preparation for the first wave of new postulants. This year I'd be a "guardian angel," helping a fresh postulant find God's Will in the Order. I'd be the one who would answer questions about the Novitiate routine and cushion the impact of the rules.

On August 15th, I became the angel for a slim, blond, cherub-faced entrant from Montana. His blue eyes opened wider with each new stop we made on our first tour of the Novitiate. I didn't know whether his silence was frozen shock or a sign that he was not very bright. Over the eight days of his postulancy, he gradually awakened from his daze and caught the drift of the daily routine. Had he moved from rural Montana to New York City, I don't think he would have been more surprised than he was at the Jesuit world in Sheridan, Oregon.

As the postulants molted into first-year novices and prepared for their long retreat, I was preparing for my first eight-day retreat. The shorter version of the Spiritual Exercises seemed as easy as a second visit to the dentist after a first one without Novocain. While the new novices were still submerged in the thirty days of their long retreat, I and the other second-year novices launched into two classes, Latin and Education, totaling six hours of academic work each week, twice as much as the year before.

EXPERIMENTS

St. Ignatius seeded the Novitiate with "experiments." Arguably, the long-retreat was our first experiment in which novices experimented with spiritual rigor. In the early days of the Order novices were sent on experiments to test their willingness to live the life demanded of Jesuits. In those times, experiments took the form of ministering to the sick in hospitals, to the poor, and to those on the fringes of society. At Sheridan in the 1950s, we second-year novices went through two experiments: serving in a retreat house in Portland and caring for a disabled Jesuit priest residing on the first floor of the Novitiate.

The Portland experiment came in short five-day bursts, during which we cleaned and prepared the rooms for the thirty or more men who came for a three-day Ignatian retreat. Scouring toilets and sinks, making beds, helping prepare meals, waiting tables, and washing dishes kept three of us moving at warp speed from 5:00 a.m. to 8:00 p.m. each day.

A vivid memory of my third day in one retreat takes me back to a rest period before the start of dinner preparation. I sat exhausted on my bed at 4:02 in the afternoon and set my alarm for the time to return to the kitchen. I fell backwards onto my pillow. The alarm buzzed me awake from a deep sleep at 4:10. Miraculously, those eight minutes carried me through the rest of that day. In a small way, I realized that, in spite of feeling out of gas, I could find a way to keep going.

The experiment with Father John McAstocker ("Father Mac"), a half-paralyzed former retreat giver, began as soon after the 5:00 a.m. wake-up bell as I could dress and get to his room. Two of us were assigned his care for a month. One would begin his month by replacing a departing novice and join the novice who had learned the routine over the prior two weeks. This revolving method always kept an experienced novice in rotation. We changed his soiled sheets (*Depends* had not yet been invented), bathed him, lifted him to the commode or to his wheelchair, helped him eat, lit his cigarette and handed it to him, and wheeled him to a specially modified altar where we would assist him as he said Mass.

I never heard Father Mac complain or utter a poor-me phrase. In my mind he was the beacon of Ignatian service, not me. He had volunteered to be our "experiment" and taught us, in the spirit of St. Ignatius, what serving others could look like.

CLEAR SAILING

By the spring of my second year, I had settled into a steady forward motion, like a standing airport traveler carried along on the belt from one gate to another. Part of the movement was the monthly chat with the novice master regarding spiritual matters. It was called a "colloquy." I hadn't experienced any ecstasies or visions, nor did I feel burdened with significant sins, serious temptations, or thoughts of leaving the Order. As far as I could tell, I had little to colloquy about. For his part, Father Elliott was a good listener, but he asked little about me personally or my spiritual life. My colloquies took the form of a brief generic chat followed by my exchanging one saint's biography for another. Of course, Jesuit saints emerged as models. I came to know there were several Jesuit saints, like St. Francis Xavier who had sailed to India, Indonesia, and Japan, where he made converts to Catholicism. I wondered what I would be called to do and whether I would experience a closeness with God.

Departures and Ending

I had no idea what others discussed with the novice master or what their spiritual journeys were. The Novitiate atmosphere censored talking with another novice about personal internal struggles. Obviously, some of my brothers had issues to discuss, because in the previous twenty months five in my class had left the Novitiate. No announcement signaled their leaving, just an empty classroom seat or a stripped bed in a cubicle. "Best to say nothing" was the unwritten rule regarding those who left. Losing an odd person didn't feel like a regrettable loss. I would say to myself, "I don't think he fit the Order very well." When it came to letting go of a friendly, bright brother, one whom I had felt comfortable working beside as a fellow servant of God, I found it hard not to dwell longer on his leaving. For him, a good fit in my mind, I had to rationalize the leaving—"He'll do well as a teacher" or "I think God has other work for him in life."

Over time, I began, in the privacy of my mind, to question that tacit rule of silence regarding those who had left. I wondered whether it was a male solution, similar to that of battle-hardened soldiers who refuse to get close to new replacements because any friend could be dead tomorrow and closeness can intensify grief and loss.

I had never seriously considered leaving the Order. It provided the high road to the priesthood and serving God with the benefit of avoiding the low road to sin and hell. An added bonus was making the journey with a great bunch of brothers.

RON'S VISIT

In June 1958, just two months before I was to pronounce my first vows, Ron arrived, having just pronounced his own first vows. Within the previous ten-day period he had graduated from dental school, finalized his enlistment in the U.S. Army, and married. Now he and his bride were driving to his first duty station in California. Father Elliott had given me permission for a two-hour afternoon visit with Ron and his wife. He drove up in our '53 Ford. I say "our" because I had chosen the car and engineered the upgrade from our '47 Ford. Of course, it was no longer "our" Ford, because I'd given him my half ownership when I entered the Novitiate.

I had not seen Ron in almost two years. He got out of the driver's seat and took three quick steps to where I was standing. He shook my hand with both of his, much like Dad. His smile was accompanied by, "How are you, big fella?"—a teasing phrase he had taken up when I became taller and heavier than him. He immediately turned, opened the passenger door, and took his wife's hand as she stepped out.

"Suzanne, I'd like you to meet my brother."

I faced a pretty, freckled redhead who added, "Pleased to meet you."

After returning the greeting, I tried to dilute what I felt certain must be the nervousness of a non-Catholic for the first time meeting a brother-in-law who wore a black dress.

"I know you must feel off balance arriving in this remote world of mine," I said, "but I wonder whether a short walk on the grounds might help you both stretch your legs after the drive down from Seattle."

The sunny day made it easy to stroll outside and chat. I tried to make Suzanne feel comfortable by asking about her family and what she looked forward to in California. After seeing the grounds, I showed them the chapel with its beautiful stained glass windows and gothic altar. Not surprisingly, Suzanne was wide-eyed, quiet, and blushed easily. Ron joked and teased me, his way of easing her awkwardness.

I let the closeness with Ron soak in. It flowed from our bond that reached across the five years that separated us. We shared the same parents, the same bedroom growing up, the same cars, and the same drive to excel at our pursuits.

The two hours were quickly gone. Ron needed to report for duty in San Francisco within forty-eight hours. I needed to observe the time limit on our visit. As Ron and Suzanne drove away I felt a warm satisfaction in the gift of my half of the car, something tangible they could use embarking on their marriage. I wondered what parallels Ron's life and mine might take in the future; he was entering the military and married life while I would formally enter the Jesuit Order in August.

CHAPTER 7

Juniorate

FIRST VOWS

As novices, we observed the vows of poverty, chastity, and obedience. Poverty meant no personal belongings, no money, and no responsibility for where the next meal was coming from. Chastity meant no dating, no sex, and no opportunity. Obedience meant following the rules, making no decisions regarding our daily schedule, what we studied, and when we could talk to one another.

"First vows" meant jumping from living "as if" I had vows to a binding Church contract. As a novice, I could leave with a simple, "I don't want to do this anymore." First vows would officially make me a Jesuit, who could add "S.J." after my name. I would not be free to walk out the door without the Order officially releasing me from my vows. First vows were a big deal.

My parents, like many others, I suppose, may have been puzzled by not being allowed to attend my vow-taking as they had attended my brother's vow-taking wedding two months before. If they were feeling left out, they never mentioned it during any of their every-three-months visits. By now, I was sure Mom had given up any plan of orchestrating my exit as she had done at St. Edward Seminary.

Entering the chapel, I felt within me a quiet, deep, odd space. It differed from the electric crackles that came with the high school graduation march. As I walked slowly with my class toward the first pew, I scanned the three stained glass windows I'd seen almost daily over the past two years. Each portrayed a Jesuit saint who stared down at me and the other novices about to take our first vows. St. Stanislaus Kostka died of poor health at the age of seventeen after only ten months in the Order; St. Aloysius Gonzaga died at twenty-three while tending the sick during a plague in Italy; St. John Berchmans died at twenty-two after exhausting himself at his studies in Rome. My age fit with these young Jesuits—I was twenty. But I was healthy and not a saint. I was here to seal the finish of the initial two-year leg of my Jesuit journey with vows of poverty, chastity, and obedience. I wondered whether those saints could look down on me from heaven today, August 15, 1958, knowing what my future would be. I knew the sequence of studies that stretched out over the next ten years, but nothing more.

I looked at the altar blazing with candles on candelabras below carved wooden spires reaching high in the apse. With the start of Mass, time slowed its march as if this ritual had become a movie viewed one frame at a time. At Communion time, we rose and solemnly walked through the open sanctuary gates up the three steps to kneel at the foot of the altar. With the celebrant facing us and holding the consecrated host aloft, one after another we pronounced aloud in Latin our vows. After my turn, I drifted into a private zone. I was standing in the middle of a large field, alert to the dead silence that often preceded sudden thunderstorms in the valley. I sensed a future, but one without edges. I'm not sure how long I was distracted, probably just a few minutes. The organ blast awakened me. The Mass and vow-taking were done. The community broke out in joyful song as we sped up our steps out of the sanctuary, through the altar gates, down the aisle, and out of the chapel.

BLINDSIDED

Succeeding in the Order meant meeting the academic standards. I winced at what greeted me at the desk of my Juniorate cubicle—Latin texts of Cicero and Livy, Plato's *Apology* in Greek, a history of Greek and Roman civilization, a book on English precepts, a first survey of English literature, Latin and Greek grammars squeezed beside Latin, Greek, and English dictionaries. I didn't think I'd fail, but worried about balancing the demands of studies with the ongoing demands of meditation and spiritual discipline.

I expected Father Basiglia's advanced Greek class would challenge me, but not what happened there. During the first day of class, I felt my breathing throttle down as if ropes had tightened around my chest. The constriction I felt contrasted sharply with the enthusiasm that bubbled out of my classmates. I sensed we dwelt in different worlds. While they raised their hands and answered in eager voices, I settled lower in my chair at the back of the small classroom holding back tears on the brink of overflowing. What was happening and where it came from was no clearer to me than the purple haze that preceded my fainting with rheumatic fever when I was six.

I'd drift away for minutes at a time. Repeatedly I'd catch myself and refocus on Father Basiglia's lecture as best I could. I looked out the window over the kitchen complex toward the brown hill a half mile away. I wasn't aware of specific rival thoughts hijacking my attention and pulling it away from the Greek at hand. I would just find myself in a dull gray place. During those first weeks as a junior, I didn't raise my hand to ask a question or volunteer an answer. Father Basiglia didn't call on me or press me to participate, although he looked directly at me when my eyes would shift back to him from my open text or from the Oregon overcast outside.

I soon realized I was falling behind in Greek and needed to ask for help to get on track. I procrastinated almost a week. Finally, during an afternoon study period, I left my second-floor cubicle for Father Basiglia's room on the first floor. The two dozen steps to his room felt like two hundred yards. I hesitated before knocking.

His barked "Yes" to my knock left me no choice but to turn the knob and step inside. I was surprised to find him in a T-shirt correcting papers at his desk while his cassock hung behind him. It was the first time I'd seen a Jesuit priest so casual.

"Brother Tracy, what brings you to my door?"

"I'm having some difficulty with the grammar in the *Apology* and can't seem to retain what we've covered."

"Is there a particular passage you're having trouble with?"

"Not really. It's just hard to hold on to what I thought I'd learned."

"Your quizzes have been OK, but not as good as I had expected."

"It's not that I'm not interested in what Plato writes, it just seems like I drift off and then the words, grammar, and thought turn into a muddy soup."

"You know, sometimes when I look at you at the back of the class, you look as if you're about to cry."

His words arrowed into me and triggered a swell of tears. I didn't want him to go any further because I didn't know what to say or where to go, and I certainly didn't want to cry in front of him. I quickly opened the *Apology*, paged to a passage, and fabricated a grammar question I already knew well enough. I needed to leave and take my muddle with me.

I never seriously considered discussing my dull heaviness with Father Keilly, the spiritual advisor assigned to juniors. His age and poor hearing made me wonder whether he would understand what was going on with me. I didn't feel the confidence in him that I had in Father Elliott, although I'd never felt like this in the Novitiate. More than my lack of confidence in Father Keilly, I doubted whether I could put into words what was going on inside me. I decided that for the present the medicines of meditation and prayer would have to cure what ailed me.

UNPLANNED LEAVE

In late September, the junior beadle stopped me as I came out of morning Latin class and told me the rector wanted to see me in his office. After leaving class books in my cubicle, I hurried down to the first-floor quarters of the rector, Father McDonald. I had never spoken to him one-on-one. He'd just recently arrived to take charge of Sheridan following his appointment as rector. His arrival had made me wonder why well-educated priests (he held a doctorate in English) were sentenced to administrative jobs. When I'd seen him walking on the grounds, his stride struck me as a glide, one that would not disturb a book were one balanced on his head. Once, when I was working in the garden, he had stopped to make good-natured small talk. He radiated gentleness.

I knocked on his door and waited for his "Come in." Stepping inside, I found him standing behind his desk, arms folded, gazing down.

As he looked up, I saw his serious look and heard the metered cadence of him saying, "Your mother called a little while ago to say your father has been hospitalized and will be going into emergency surgery. The doctors say it's serious, but not much else is known. I think it's best that you go to Seattle. You'll need to pack and get away right after lunch. Brother Donovan can drive you to the bus in McMinnville, which will take you to the Greyhound station in Portland. Buses leave there several times a day for Seattle. Do you have any questions?"

I stood frozen. *Mom and Dad visited me in May and they both looked fine. Was Dad going to die? What happened? Dad has always been strong. How's Mom doing?* As worries gnawed away at me, my mind flashed back two years to October 1956 when Grandma Bury had died, and I couldn't attend her funeral because leaving Sheridan was restricted to emergencies within the "immediate family." Dad now qualified.

I'd not been away from the building overnight in over two years except for the experiments at the retreat house in Portland the year before. I made my way to the "common closet" that held a hodge-podge of clothes beyond the two cassocks we called our own. There I assembled a clerical outfit—a black suit and black shirt fitted with a Roman collar, attire I'd never worn before. Father McDonald sent word that I was to stay at the Jesuit residence at Seattle Prep, where the rector there would decide when I was to return to Sheridan.

After lunch, I met Brother Donovan in the carport and we eased away in the four-door Chevy Bel Air. The car's bright yellow had always struck me as a bit flashy for an Order that vowed poverty, but Jesuits didn't get to choose the color of donated vehicles. We wove our way down the gravel road past the outdoor basketball court and newly built handball courts. Fat heifers close to the road eyed us from the field where they grazed, a fence separating them from the acres of plum trees just recently picked. I felt the Chevy accelerate once the Novitiate's gravel road gave way to Yamhill County's blacktop. My mind sped ahead to what I might find myself later that day. Numbness and the smooth sway of the car fogged over my fear of Dad dying.

THE HOSPITAL

In Seattle's small, dilapidated, red-bricked Greyhound Station on Stewart Street I waited for Mom to pick me up and take me to Providence Hospital. My black raincoat, small black fedora, and Roman collar must have had magical power that awakened the grizzled gentleman dozing on a worn wooden bench in the waiting area. When I came within a few feet of him, he snapped full awake. His bloodshot eyes, unshaven face, and raspy voice asking for a quarter, fit my dad's description of someone "down-on-his-luck." I tried, as respectfully as I could, to say I had no spare money, not knowing whether I was free to give away any of the few dollar bills and change from the twenty-dollars I was given for bus tickets. He took my refusal well, adding, "Thanks anyway, Father."

"Father" reverberated in my head and set off a wave of silent protests: *I'm just a few months past twenty. Was he using flattery to see whether that would get money? Or does this clerical outfit make me look older? I'm a make-believe priest.* Through the station's glass doors I caught sight of Mom in the family Pontiac pulled up to the curb. I quickly moved to the car.

It was early evening. Mom looked haggard and serious. Right away she launched into a summary of the surgery that had finished mid-afternoon. She said Ron had flown in from basic Army training in Texas. She perked up while relating that the primary surgeon, who also was the family doctor, had asked Ron whether he wanted to scrub up and observe the surgery up close. Mom beamed as she related how Ron watched two surgeons open Dad's abdomen and begin the four-hour procedure. Ron later told me that several times he had looked around the hood, separating Dad's upper body from the operating field, to check Dad's breathing even though the anesthesiologist was monitoring it. My brother's cool spectator role didn't strike me as unusual, just vintage Ron—he could distance himself from his feelings just as he did when hitting a difficult golf shot. While not squeamish, I stiffened at the thought of watching surgeons carve up my father.

Mom related how both the surgeon and Ron had told her how well Dad tolerated the removal of a tumor from his colon. She said the doctor would give the four of us a run-down on the findings in the morning.

Providence Hospital was quieter than I had expected. Physicians' quick steps and nurses' fixed eyes signaled a reverent focus on where they were going. Providence nuns, the same Order that had taught me at St. Catherine's, were silent except for the chatter of the long rosaries that hung from their waists.

Dad was sleeping when Mom and I came into the room. The hospital bed slightly elevated his head and torso. His ashen face and closed eyes looked coffin-ready. Were it not for the tubing in his nose and mouth that snaked to wheezing machines beside him, I'd have thought he had passed away. Mom's hand on Ron's shoulder stirred him out of catnapping in the chair pulled close to Dad's bed. Ron was catching up on the sleep he'd lost on his early flight from Texas. Without a word, we moved into the hall and discussed a plan between then and the next morning's meeting with the surgeon. Ron and I pressured and cajoled Mom into going home where both she and he could try to get deserved sleep. I argued and won the battle to stay with Dad through the night.

Around 10:00 that night, an apparition drifted into my twilight doze. A Providence nun in an all-white habit stood a few feet in front of me. I realized then that Providence nuns who were nurses wore all white and not the black-and-white of teaching nuns I was used to.

"Mr. Tracy, what are your plans for tonight?"

"I thought I'd just sit here with my father through the night."

"He's resting nicely and I don't think he'll awaken tonight."

"I'd feel better being close to him."

With that, the nun-in-white smiled and quietly left.

To keep sleep at bay I began to inventory the machines and figure out their functions as they hummed and beeped with Dad's breathing.

"Mr. Tracy," awakened me. The nun-in-white stood just inside the door.

I looked at my watch, 11:05 p.m. I'd lost the battle to stay awake.

"I've arranged a room just down the hall where you can sleep. I'll let you know if there are any changes in your father's status."

With an "OK," I surrendered to common sense and followed her to a private room where a small lamp cast its light on the high-standing hospital bed.

"There will be a Mass said in the main chapel at 6:30 in the morning."

"I'd appreciate it if someone could wake me at six," I replied.

"I'll make sure someone does." And she was gone.

Mom and Ron arrived shortly after 10:00 the next morning to find me sitting quietly with Dad, who'd managed to drink some tea and complain about being offered Jell-O for breakfast. After asking Dad about his night and making sure he'd been properly treated (he omitted his Jell-O complaint), Mom asked me how I felt after being up all night. I confessed that I'd had a good night's sleep, thanks to an angel who had turned out to be a nun. She smiled approvingly and then asked Ron about his training at Fort Sam Houston. She followed his answers with questions about what I was studying in the Juniorate. We all knew we were filling time before the main event of the day—our meeting with the surgeon, who would come by after making his morning rounds.

"Preliminary results indicate the tumor was colon cancer," Dr. Sauntry said.

The room was eerily quiet. My jaw tightened and my stomach knotted. Somehow I'd naively taken in Mom's upbeat mood and perkiness the night before and used them to play down how serious Dad's situation really was.

As Ron prepared to return to basic training in Texas, my curiosity led me to ask about his Army training.

"What do dentists do in their basic training?" I said.

"We start by doing a lot of what raw recruits do."

"Like what?"

"We march, we learn to fire weapons, and answer, 'Yes, sir.'"

"It sounds like you have your novitiate too,"

"I like learning how to use a rifle and a pistol."

"What don't you like?"

"I don't like crawling on my stomach under barbed wire with live rounds whizzing by not far above my head."

"I guess we all have our penance."

"The best news is I'm being assigned stateside to a medical unit at the Presidio in San Francisco."

"I'll have to study a few more years before I get assigned to teaching," I said.

The next week, after Ron had returned to Army training, Dad, Mom, and I met in Dr. Sauntry's office. This time he shared the technical laboratory analysis that determined that the tumor was Stage III adenocarcinoma of the transverse colon. Follow-up consisted of "monitoring" Dad's progress.

I came away from the doctor's office with the same confident faith in 1950's medicine as I had in Catholicism shepherded by Pope Pius XII, who died a few weeks later. Growing up, I'd put physicians on a pedestal just below priests, confident that neither group made mistakes.

With Dad's discharge from the hospital, I returned to Sheridan to resume my studies. I reflexively relied on prayer and God's will to care for Dad. In Greek class I moved to a vacant seat in the second row and away from the window. I'd resolved to clear the dull haze that had plagued me before my trip home. I realized I was not equipped to figure out what was going on inside me after taking vows and officially becoming a Jesuit. Only much later did I recognize the smoldering sadness I quarantined then as I had done before with other loose ends in the previous two years. I pushed forward by picking up the familiar Jesuit banner inscribed with *Age quod agis.* It was a mantra that steered me back to studying Greek, Latin, speech, and two courses in English.

FATHER DEMPSEY

The survey of English Literature offered me a departure from the rote learning of translating Latin and Greek. A required book report demanded that I offer a personal reaction and give an opinion. Thus far, the Order had not tutored me in expressing what I thought. Besides, I was afraid of missing the point in what I read and embarrassing myself.

I walked down to the first floor and crossed the brightly buffed hallway outside the chapel to the cement stairs leading to the lowest level in the building, a basement really. From the stairs it was just a few steps to Father Dempsey's room and office. Had I been blind, my nose would have led me toward the musty smell of cigarettes past and present, the signature sign of this chunky, stately, and chain-smoking Jesuit professor. He held two master's degrees from Yale, one in English and the other in speech. He was intimidating, opinionated, and often hard to figure out. This was my first private meeting with him. I was coming to deliver my book report on Charles Dickens' *David Copperfield.* My knock brought his husky, "Turn the knob and push."

Just inside the door to the right, a tilted stack of *New York Times* Sunday editions rose three feet from the floor. All flat surfaces—his desk, chair seats, tops of boxes, and half of the floor—were blanketed with papers, periodicals, and books not accommodated by the bookcases on three sides of the room. Putting his cigarette carefully in the closer of two ashtrays, he rose from behind his desk and cleared a straight-back chair. As he sat down he reached for his still burning Chesterfield. Both my parents had smoked, but I don't ever recall being in a small sealed room, or even in a car, where the smoke penetrated nostrils, lungs, and clothes as quickly and as thoroughly as it did in Father Dempsey's room.

"I'm turning in my book report and am ready for another book," I began.

"Let me have a look at it." And with that he took my two typed pages and eased back in his chair. He slipped off his glasses and cleaned each lens with a circular rub of his bare index finger, a motion that could only more evenly distribute the film. After what seemed ten minutes, but likely was three, he asked, "Do you really think that Dickens was addressing social conditions in England?"

"I do."

He rolled his eyes skeptically while *Did I really completely miss the boat?* swirled in my head.

I added, "I thought much of what he wrote paralleled the conditions found in his *Christmas Carol* where Ebenezer Scrooge was exploiting Bob Cratchit."

"Do you really think the social conditions in England played a major role in the book?" he repeated.

"Well, yes."

Looking down at his cigarette, which by now had a precarious one-inch ash, he picked it up and stretched his arm to the second ashtray where he deftly broke off the ash to join several identical ash spirals that had formed a rising pyramid.

"Regarding your next book, I think Charlotte Bronte's *Jane Eyre* would be a good next read."

I came away wondering whether I'd misread Dickens or whether Father Dempsey was putting me to a test. I wanted to hear his opinion and reasoning rather than just his skeptical tone and repeated question. As I climbed the stairs back to my cubicle, I thought of the clear opinions he'd breezily tossed out in class—a dismissal of Ernest Hemingway with, "His writing is marked by a hairy-chested approach to life," his brushing aside the poetry of Walt Whitman with, "Poor prose masquerading as poetry," and his eulogizing Shakespeare as the "Unmatched master of human nature and the English language." I wondered whether his queries with me were Jesuitical equivocations meant to prod me to think more deeply or genuine skepticism of my comprehension.

I felt a growing tension that came out in deep breaths and a flurry of internal questions: *Why do we spend almost all our time translating Horace and Homer and almost none on the themes and meaning behind what they're saying? Are we just expected to repeat what we hear? Why aren't we encouraged to form opinions, discuss them, debate them? Why are there such tight reins on us? Or is it me? Is it my shortcoming?*

I had questions about my spiritual life too. *Is this the work of the devil stirring unrest that Ignatius warns us about in the Spiritual Exercises? Who can I talk to? Not to my brothers, not to Father Keilly, to no one?* I returned to the standing advice of St. Ignatius—*Age quod agis.*

FAMILY VISIT

My parents came for a visit in January, the first in eight months. Dad's cancer had thrown off the rhythm of their visits. Scanning

Dad's face, I saw that his hospital cadaver-gray complexion was gone, succeeded by the ruddy pink that comes from work outside checking railroad cars. Mom began talking as fast as a teletype machine pumping out news stories.

When she got to, "Fidel Castro took over Cuba at the beginning of the month after he drove Batista from power," I broke in with, "We became aware of that because in the Juniorate we now have a few news stories clipped from the Portland *Oregonian* and pinned on our bulletin board each week."

"What do you think of the new Pope, John XXIII?" I added.

"He seems pretty old for the job," Mom replied.

"Yes, he's pretty close to eighty."

"I read in the *Progress* that he is a 'caretaker' pope, an interim pope not expected to do much."

Neither of us knew how revolutionary Castro and John XXIII were, how close to war the Cuban missile crisis would take the world, how many reforms Vatican II would attempt to make in the Church.

Dad stepped in, "Ethel, tell Jim what you've done."

"Well, the insurance payment from your father's surgery allowed us to pull together $1200. I convinced the knitting instructor at Frederick's to match that amount and come in with me to start our own knitting store with me in charge of the business end. I found a space just on the edge of the new Bellevue Mall, which is huge and draws good customers who live on the east side of Lake Washington. The location of our shop saves them a drive across the floating bridge into downtown Seattle. We opened last month just in time for the Christmas rush. I also got ahold of the same yarn salesmen who sold to Frederick's and worked the same discounts. My goal is to pay off the house in two years."

As Mom talked, I flashed back to the expression on her face after the doctor announced Dad's cancer diagnosis. I recalled her unblinking, steel, agate-blue eyes locking on a target. Now I saw her bull's-eye as financial security. She was determined. I knew she would be successful.

An Uplift

The summer of 1959 arrived and with it came a second course in French, together with a course entitled *An Introduction to Education*. I liked them both. I loved the sound of French and enjoyed the lilt that made me sometimes feel the buttery French slide off the tongue—*aujourd'hui* so much smoother than "today." But the education course gripped me more. I still find Father Weller, the teacher, a vivid presence in my mind, but not his face, voice, or gestures. More than fifty years have erased myriad memories and smudged others. He may have had thinning hair and worn glasses, but I'm not confident those fragments are accurate. What remains are the goading questions he posed in class.

"If the word 'school' comes from the Greek word for 'leisure' (σχολή), what's the connection?"

"What did Aristotle think 'leisure' was for?"

"How do we, as educators, help students see that 'leisure' is more than just a break from 'work'?"

He laid out his vision for the Jesuit specialty of teaching as knowing oneself, stimulating the mind, and introducing students to the pursuit of truth. He freed my quarantined frustration with only translating Greek and Roman ideas and offered an exciting alternative. He prodded us with the Greek dictum— γνῶθι σεαυτόν (Know yourself), and woke me up to how many meanings it had, and how little I knew about myself.

Father Weller's classes lit a fuse of lively discussions that spread into evening recreation. These rapid-fire exchanges prompted good-natured chiding from brothers who weren't interested in wasting after-dinner leisure this way. Both Brother Marsh and I discussed and reveled in what Father Weller was advocating.

A PACKAGE

During the annual eight-day retreat in the fall of 1959, I returned to my cubicle from the chapel, where I'd been meditating. On my desk was a small package, its brown paper wrapping sealed tight with cellophane tape. The round, black printing spelling out my address, together with the return Army address of the Presidio in San Francisco, signaled a surprise from my brother. Opening the package, I found three paperbacks—Allen Ginsberg's *Howl,* Jack Kerouac's *On the Road,* and Lawrence Ferlinghetti's *A Coney Island of the Mind.* I pulled out the three-by-five card peeking out of one of the books—just three words, "Happy reading. Ron." Guessing that the package had been delivered by mistake, because mail was never delivered during retreats, I put the books and wrapping paper on top of the already full book shelf on my desk. I knew only spiritual reading was proper during retreats. I knew these books had to be turned in to the library. I sat down and wrote out my reflections on the meditation I'd just finished.

In the evening, when I came back from a walk outside, the substitute for after-supper recreation, I immediately noticed the books and wrapping paper were gone. *That's weird.*

With the end of the retreat, the beadle delivered a note saying Father Adams wanted to see me. I was surprised by the summons. He was not a teacher. I had never spoken to him and only knew him as "Father Minister." His role was to attend to the community's material needs: keeping the lights on, the heat on, and the cows fed, among the many tasks necessary to run our satellite branch of Gonzaga University. I knew Father

Adams most clearly as the priest, in khaki pants and a woolen coat, riding his motorcycle, with its empty sidecar, down the road to the barns.

When Father Adams opened his door after one knock, he got right to the point.

"Brother Tracy, I found books in your cubicle that shouldn't have been delivered. The brother who picked up the mail forgot to hold it back until the end of retreat. That's why I went to all cubicles to pick up the delivered mail. When I found those books in your cubicle and opened, I took them to Father Taylor, who said he wants to see you."

With growing apprehension, I left for the first-floor room of Father Taylor, who was in charge of the library.

"Brother Tracy, why didn't you turn in those unauthorized books when you first received them?" Father Taylor began.

"I thought because it was retreat time, I'd maintain silence and would turn them in after the retreat ended."

"Did you read any of the books?"

"No, I didn't."

Father Taylor looked directly at me and met my unblinking eyes in return.

"Are you acquainted with the nature of those books?"

"I didn't recognize any of the authors' names. In one of my brother's letters he wrote about some new popular writers in San Francisco where he's living. I think he called them part of the 'Beat Generation.'"

"But you didn't read any of the books?"

"No, I didn't."

I left Father Taylor's room hurt and frustrated, but clear-headed enough to know not to ask whether I could have the books back to read. I trolled for guilt, but found no evidence regarding reading. I had to go back to the time or two in grade school when I had read comic books under my bedcovers by flashlight when I was supposed to be asleep. I was sure the Beats were different from what I'd been reading recently— Chaucer, Milton, Shakespeare.

The quizzing made me think of the *Index Librorum Prohibitorum* (The Index of Prohibited Books) begun in the mid-1550's, populated with titles the Church had judged to be immoral or embracing a theological error. The Index still lolled around in 1959, and included books by Copernicus, Descartes, Erasmus, Galileo, Kant, Jonathan Swift, and even Graham Greene. The little I'd heard in the Order about this list of not-to-be-read books was that it was not taken seriously. But it still existed. And if it existed, I knew someone must be taking it seriously.

Negative thoughts and feelings rattled around inside me: hurt that Father Adams and Father Taylor might think I was sneaking around reading illicit, terrible stuff; frustration that I needed to be fed the filtered and pureed proper diet of literature. Both reactions made me acutely aware that distrust easily grows when you don't know a person. Neither priest really knew me.

During my examination of conscience that evening I concluded that, like the Beats' books, my critical thoughts and resentful feeling needed to be expurgated. I never saw the books again and never found them listed in the library's card catalogue.

PROMOTIONS

The surprise promotion of Father McDonald to provincial of the five-state Oregon Province led to the surprise appointment of Father Taylor, vigilant librarian and classics professor, as interim rector. I was doubly surprised a few weeks later when Father Taylor appointed me beadle for the fifty juniors. I felt uneasy not knowing whether I'd measure up to new rector's stickler style, especially in the light of his earlier inquisition of me for harboring Beat Generation books. I was further surprised how his uptight manner morphed into a friendlier more relaxed one punctuated with a few smiles. Even his black oxfords, known for their rhythmic squeak when he walked down the hall, seem to have fallen silent.

As beadle for the next six months I'd relay the rector's directives to my peers. I'd carry out the day-to-day duties of ringing the bell for lights out, posting jobs, and starting and stopping the *flagellatio*.

THE LIGHTER SIDE

Father Taylor's newly found easy-going manner didn't go untested. He was proud of garnering for the library rare Greek and Latin books and manuscripts, as well as artifacts. He housed the artifacts in glass display cases donated by a Portland department store. He was especially proud of the ancient coins he had found while studying in Italy. He told us how he had located areas inhabited in early Roman times that now were farmland. In the early spring, after a heavy rainfall had drenched the freshly plowed fields, he'd walk the rows and occasionally find an ancient coin or broken pottery the rain had uncovered. The Roman booty now was proudly displayed each with a card indicating the type of pottery or the year the coin was minted.

While Father Taylor was away on his annual retreat, the junior head librarian put the finishing touches on the last display case.

Having heard that the displays were finally complete, a group of faculty members came to view Father Taylor's finished project. Chuckles broke out at two displays nested in the display cases. One featured the bottom rear-half of an old shoe, with the typed descriptor, "Achilles' Heel." The other, a rumpled burlap potato bag, was headlined as "The Sack of Rome."

A leak from one faculty member led us to conclude that the reason Father Taylor never mentioned the prank was the good-natured advice fellow professors gave him upon his return. Practical jokes among us diluted the serious and rigid routine of the Order. They intertwined more strands in the bond of brotherhood.

THE TERM PAPER
The final semester of the Juniorate brought a second course in European history. The course challenged us to write the longest, most thorough paper up to this point in our studies. I still rode the wave of the Jesuit educational ideals Father Weller had triggered during summer school. I shopped for a historical figure I could admire, one who fit the portrait Father Weller had sketched.

I found it hard to put down Johan Huizinga's book to get back to my other subjects, I knew I'd chosen the subject of my term paper—Desiderius Erasmus Roterodamus (1466-1536), aka Erasmus. From my reading, this illegitimate son of a priest had survived being orphaned and forced by circumstances into a monastery, a route that eventually led him to the priesthood. Erasmus mastered Latin and Greek, and blossomed into a world-famous scholar. His scholarship helped him finagle from the pope release from priestly obligations. While Huizinga didn't paint Erasmus as perfect, his openness and honesty shone through. His criticism of theologians and the Church, found in his *In Praise of Folly*, predated the outbreak of Luther's challenges to the corruption within the Catholic Church. Erasmus agreed with Luther's criticisms of Church abuses. He corresponded in a collegial way with Luther and other critics of the Church. His cool head eventually earned him Luther's wrath for not joining forces with him in breaking away from the Church of Rome. Erasmus seemed to float above the anger at Church abuses that played a role in the formation of Protestant churches. His scholarship struck me as moving in tandem with a steady, balanced personality. In spite of his keen awareness of the Church's shortcomings, he never broke with the Vatican. Eventually, his unflagging writing and energy earned him fame as an accomplished theologian.

Erasmus hobnobbed with major figures of the sixteenth century. He knew the young Henry VIII before he became king, and won the friendship of Thomas More before Henry VIII removed More's head. My sampling of his writing revealed a sharp tongue and a sense of humor. Had he lived long enough to meet and come under the spell of Ignatius, I was sure he would have become a Jesuit. He stood as a model of what I wanted to become. He ranked with the best of his contemporaries in honesty—open, balanced, and always eager to learn. I found it disheartening and ironic that after his death the Church put his books on the *Index of Forbidden Books.*

For my research, Father Taylor gave me access to rare books, the kind that crackled when you opened them and released the musty smell that only paper a few centuries old gives off. I handled the books as carefully as the chalices I touched in the sacristy. I felt a reverent enthusiasm as I searched and copied references and quotations on three-by-five cards. I felt satisfied creating a hub thesis and organizing the spokes of argument. The actual writing was the least satisfying element, if I don't count typing the final product and two carbon copies on a clunky Underwood typewriter. Quite proud of my paper and confident of earning a good grade, I submitted my *Magnum Opus.*

The father professor wrote a few bland comments about the content and structure of the paper. He did, however, heavily criticize the mistyping one Latin quotation from Erasmus. The sloppy citation appeared to have carried most of weight in the final grade, C. I tried to console myself with having found Erasmus and what he stood for.

Moving On

In the spring of 1960, I began to look forward to finishing my four years at Sheridan and moving on to philosophy, which offered a chance for young Jesuits to spread their wings. With philosophy came the option to take courses outside the priestly track, ones that eventually could lead to a master's or a doctoral degree necessary for teaching college. Already several of my peers had zeroed in on English, economics, and mathematics. I thought and prayed about what specialty I'd like to pursue in the Order.

I'd been feeling a growing desire to help people in more than a spiritual way. I wanted to master how the mind develops, what motivates us, where emotions spring from, and why we make particular choices. I'd never read a psychology book or taken a psychology course. Even more mysterious was my interest in psychiatry, which, like psychology, I'd never studied or knew much about other than it required completion of medical school before residency training.

Like knowing at age ten that I wanted to carry newspapers, at thirteen to enroll at St. Edward Seminary, and at seventeen to enter the Society, this goal arrived stamped with a felt sense of certainty. Helping others psychologically through psychiatry just felt right. The conviction raced my pulse as if I'd found a gold nugget the size of a fist.

I knew Father Kaufmann, the Province dean of studies, was coming in May to interview each of us moving on to philosophy. He would discuss and scrutinize our special interests.

As I waited in the queue outside Father Kaufman's interview room, I braced for resistance to what I was sure he would see as a harebrained idea. I didn't know of any Jesuit who was a physician, and the Oregon Province had fewer than five Ph.D.'s in psychology.

Finally, it was my turn to face Father Kaufman, who was still jotting notes from the prior interview when I sat down. As he put down his pen and looked up, I scanned his oval face. I'd never spoken with him. I'd not talked to many priests in the Order with power over my future.

"And tell me, Brother Tracy, what long-term course of studies are you interested in?" he asked.

After a covert deep breath, I launched into my interest in psychiatry and how it fit into the role I eventually would like to have as a Jesuit ministering to souls and psyches. Less than five sentences into my request, he broke in.

"It will take a lot of science to complete pre-med studies."

"I understand that."

"Are you up to it?"

"Yes, I think so."

And with that brief exchange he dismissed me matter-of-factly, as if I made a simple request like, "May I have a new pair of shoes?" Father Kaufman had neither challenged my goal nor acted as if it were a crazy idea. I left the room befuddled. His questions seemed geared at testing my seriousness and not rejecting the idea, as I had thought he would.

Within a month, I'd received notice that I would not be spending the final summer school in the Juniorate again studying French. I was to move two months ahead of my class to Mount St. Michael in Spokane, where I'd be commuting to Gonzaga University for a course in organic chemistry, a first step in pre-med studies.

The final weeks in the Juniorate sped by. Thoughts of my four years at Sheridan kept breaking into my morning meditations. I shelved the ups-and-downs that had cycled through me. I knew that life at Mount St. Michael, summer school in science, and three years of philosophy would carry me further in the Order. I hoped each step forward would be better than the last.

CHAPTER 8

Mount St. Michael

The Volkswagen van's low gear growled up the steep road to Mount St. Michael outside Spokane, Washington. I gazed at the red-brick seminary sprawled across the crest of a hill dotted with a few maple trees and grass losing its fight to the brown that comes with dry summers. The van's open window offered little breeze and no relief from the mid-90's heat. This move to Mount St. Michael was much more than a car ride. I was moving to the third plateau of the five needed to become a Jesuit priest. Newly ordained Jesuits often stopped at Sheridan on their way north to Washington and encouraged us, who had nine years or more of study and work before ordination. Like runners who had already finished the marathon, they came back to us, still on the course, to cheer us with words like, "The Latin and Greek are tough, but philosophy is great, and theology is the best." I believed their words and looked forward to the fall start of philosophy.

SUMMER 1960

The organic chemistry of summer school ramped up my excitement over taking the first step on a pre-med program. However, I did feel uneasy knowing I had not completed the prerequisite general chemistry courses, although I had taken high school chemistry.

The Monday after arriving at the Mount, I rode the seminary's bus to the Gonzaga campus, where five days a week I was to devote my waking hours to organic chemistry. Timothy O'Leary, S.J., the teacher, held an Ohio State Ph.D. in chemistry and was known as "Grim Tim" for his quiet serious manner and tough grading. It was said that he was harder on Jesuit students because he didn't want anyone to get the impression that he gave breaks to his brothers in Christ. My classmate Dahlquist who wanted to teach chemistry, also came early to the Mount. We discovered that calling each other "Brother" was left behind at Sheridan. Last names now sufficed.

I shouldered into the five-days-a-week grind of lectures, labs, and quizzes on campus. Back at the Mount in the afternoons, I studied in my room, which was the middle-third of a sub-divided second-floor classroom facing west. Paper thin walls separated me from the makeshift storage rooms on either side. Although I pulled down the stiff, tan shades over the three eight-foot-high windows, the summer sun relentlessly raised the temperature. There was no air-conditioning. No breeze entered the open window. To cope with the heat, I gave myself permission to strip off the roasting cassock and work at my desk in slacks and T-shirt. I tried not to let the dripping sweat stain the text or my homework paper.

WORLDLY SHIFTS

During the initial week of classes, I made my first visit to the Mount St. Michael outdoor swimming pool. I looked forward to it as a perfect one-hour break following the bus ride back from Gonzaga before starting chemistry homework. Swimming ushered in a world markedly different from the vacuum-sealed Novitiate and Juniorate of the previous four years.

Mount St. Michael, Spokane, Washington
(Jesuit Oregon Province Archives)

The first time I opened the gate of the whitewashed wooden fence surrounding the Mount's swimming pool, I saw no one in the water, but did notice a few dozing second- and third-year philosophers on their stomachs soaking up the sun like beached seals. Squinting to dampen the sun's glare off the water, I dropped my towel on a lawn chair at the pool's edge and dove into the water. As I surfaced and rolled over on my back, I caught the words and music from a radio beside a snoozing Jesuit. "She wore an itsy bitsy teeny-weeny yellow polka-dot bikini." Four years had passed since I had heard popular music. *How am I going to fit this into my life of celibacy?*

It took me almost two days and two meditations to figure out that it's one thing to troll for songs with sexual innuendos and quite another to occasionally come across a popular song with a catchy beat and a sexy allusion. If I was going to avoid everything with a whiff of sexuality, I'd have to pass over passages in the New Testament about Mary Magdalen and never again read *Romeo and Juliet*.

A sunbaked Saturday brought a welcome midsummer break from chemistry. I was helping clean out a shed behind the main seminary building. I liked swinging a hammer and crow-barring apart wood pallets. I felt refreshed by the sweat that came with physical work outside, very different from the sweat that spilled out of me in the sauna of my room. I worked alongside Casey and Kaniecki, both entering their third and last year of philosophy. Casey stood at least five inches over six feet, an asset to his athleticism that had earned him a basketball scholarship to Seattle University before he entered the Order. Kaniecki, on the other hand, was built like a linebacker for the Detroit Lions, the football team representing his hometown. I'd learned that he'd chosen to join the Oregon Province of the Jesuits, rather than a province in the East, because he wanted to become a missionary in Alaska.

"Kaniecki, don't you think it's about time to load up the truck and take this stuff to the dump?" Casey asked mid-afternoon.

"You know, I think the scrap metal at the back of the shed should go on the bottom of the load," replied Kaniecki. "We could drop off the wood at the dump and take the metal to the scrap place in town."

"That's a great idea. Tracy, do you want to ride along, get off the hill for a while, and cool off?" Kaniecki asked.

"Sure," I said.

I'd not been away from Mount St. Michael except for the bus rides to class at Gonzaga. I sat between the two of them as Casey started the Mount's small Chevy truck. We all wore Levis and shirts grimy from work and damp from sweat. We looked like what my dad called "working stiffs."

I had no idea where the dump or the scrap metal drop-off was. I just liked the idea of going for an unplanned ride. Casey coasted most of the way down the hill from the Mount and within twenty minutes had found the two destinations where we disposed of the wood and metal. The distance we'd come struck me as a long way to travel for such a small load. With the truck emptied of its load, Casey turned toward downtown Spokane driving west past Gonzaga. Not far from Spokane Falls he pulled into a parking lot off Broadway and Lincoln.

Without a word, the elder philosophers got out of the cab and crossed the street toward a four-story redbrick building with a corner tower that rose to five stories. I got out and tagged along. My companions strolled to a small stairway. As I climbed the five steps behind them to a glass-paned door, I read the sign painted on the wall above it: "Welcome to the Rainer Brewery Tasting Room."

We didn't have to take the brewery tour to enjoy the complimentary beer, the first beer I'd drunk in over four years. I enjoyed sitting quietly sipping the beer. I wondered how many times Casey and Kaniecki had visited the tasting room. We didn't talk about the trip, the destination, or the beer. We simply rode back to the Mount, tidied up the shed we'd cleaned out, and put away the tools.

As I did with a lot of unexpected events in the Order, I privately tried to fit this visit into the religious life. I didn't think what we'd done was "scandalous," a word reserved for describing behavior far outside the boundary of our calling to be Jesuits. "Puzzling" and "off-kilter" fit better, similar to the "itsy bitsy teeny-weeny yellow polka-dot bikini" that had rattled me at the swimming pool.

The end of summer school opened the door to a two-week vacation break at Hayden Lake in the north panhandle of Idaho. There the Jesuits owned several acres of forested land, where they'd sprinkled eight-man Army-surplus tents mounted atop wooden platforms. The tents served as sleeping quarters that ringed the single wooden building housing a kitchen, dining area, and chapel-meeting room. On clear days the rising sun shot shafts of light between the tall evergreens and turned the early morning mist translucent. The scene looked like one of the devotional pictures I'd seen in religious books, except this scene was real. It even enriched my morning meditation.

However, when it rained—and unfortunately it did for several days during those two weeks of August—chill penetrated the skin and took up residence deep in my body. After lunch on the third rainy day, shivers prompted me to scan the shelves of books in the main building's alcove. With just a cursory glance I grabbed a paperback and headed for the tent. Cocooned in the blankets on my cot next to the tent's entry flap opened for light, I read my first self-selected novel as a Jesuit, John Steinbeck's *Cannery Row*. Steinbeck's writing and the warmth of the blankets tight around me made me lose myself in the story and forget the cold. The freedom to select a novel felt foreign, almost wrong, as if I'd picked a forbidden fruit. I felt the grip of the previous four years loosen.

Brothers Separated and Gained

With the end of vacation, I returned to the Mount, where most of my class had arrived from Sheridan. I say "most" because Frank, my buddy in high school who had become my brother in the Order, was assigned to study philosophy in St. Louis. I would miss his wry smile, his wit, and his unflappable steadiness. Yet I was confident that we would be companions again perhaps three years ahead in regency or in theology six years down the road.

In addition to my classmates from Oregon, first-year philosophers streamed in from Canada and California. The Canadians had completed their Novitiate and Juniorate 1,800 miles away in Guelph, Ontario, while the Californians had run a parallel path in Los Gatos, 750 miles south. The common background we shared made it easier to meet and mingle. A few U.S. Jesuits began to rib the Canucks by ending their sentences with an "Ay." The Canadians, of course, bantered back with "Oh, you Yanks." Beneath the humor and jokes, the Jesuit camaraderie blended our diverse group into a band focused on philosophy under the banner of Christ and His Church.

The annual eight-day retreat further fused us together and preambled the approaching school year. Because all of us had gone through the Spiritual Exercises several times, a fresh director from outside the community was brought in to conduct it. I saw his job as daunting. He was expected to compress the spiritual dynamism of an Ignatian four-week retreat into eight days. He did his best to emphasize the later weeks of the retreat, but no Ignatian retreat director could omit the first week. He was no exception. The four retreats

I'd been through had taught me to accept the Exercise's first week dose of self-loathing and the punishment I deserved for my past sinfulness. It was as if I'd been taught to suppress the reflex to block an expected punch in the face.

THE SCHOOL YEAR BEGINS

An enthusiastic Jesuit professor, who had recently earned his doctorate in philosophy, opened the first day of class with, "The Philosophy of Being (metaphysics) is the most fundamental course in philosophy." And with that he tossed us first-year philosophers into the brambles of *being, essence, substance, accidents, form,* and *prime matter*—all terms gleaned from Aristotle, perpetuated by Thomas Aquinas, and consolidated into a twentieth-century textbook. Over the course of the first semester, I grew disheartened with my futile attempts to firmly grasp the eel of "being as being." I managed to memorize elements of metaphysics, but failed to find its relevance. During that first year only two courses made sense to me—*Introduction to Philosophy* and *Logic.*

Father O'Leary's two-semester course in general chemistry, which had begun with Gonzaga's fall semester, helped offset the drag of philosophy. It even allowed me and other Jesuits in chemistry to take the required laboratory experiments at the Mount, because it had a small laboratory. Dahlquist had struggled with the summer course in organic chemistry, but maintained his plodding determination. Mr. David Clarke, a scholastic being fast-tracked through the ordinary fourteen-year gauntlet of Jesuit training, oversaw our chemistry labs because he had earned a doctorate in chemistry prior to entering the Order. He now was completing his fourth phase of Jesuit training, regency, by teaching science courses at the Mount. And like all teaching scholastics, he was addressed as "Mr. Clarke."

Mr. Clarke was a big man. While he may have only been six-feet tall, his considerable girth and impish smile made me immediately recall the colored pictures of Falstaff I'd seen in bound volumes of Shakespeare's plays. Mr. Clarke wore thick glasses and displayed a mellow sense of humor. He bounced on his toes while eagerly sharing his wide interest in the sciences. His current science favorite was geology. His enthusiasm for the study of the solid earth partly came from the fact that he was in charge of the seismograph planted in the volcanic rock beneath the Mount. Prior to his conducting our first experiment in the chemistry lab, perhaps as an excuse to showcase a pet interest, he led me and four other philosopher-chemistry students down into the bowels of the sprawling building. We had to round our shoulders and duck our heads to keep from hitting the low-hanging floor above us. We walked carefully on the slippery shale to reach the plywood door of the twelve-foot-square room that housed the seismograph. Inside we saw close up the needles tracing the earth's jitters on slowly streaming paper. Pinned on the wall, three-foot lengths of paper displayed evidence of prior quakes with dark lines so close they looked like inkblots. If the Mount had possessed a telescope, I'm sure Mr. Clarke would have taken us to the roof to gaze at the stars. He lit for me a fuse of eagerness to know the world through the curious and questioning eyes of science.

PHILOSOPHY COMES ALIVE

In the second year at the Mount, I began to gain traction in philosophy. The *Philosophy of Man* and the *Philosophy of Science* carried me out of the arid dunes of "being as being" and the metaphysics of Aristotle. I got acquainted with medieval Thomas Aquinas, together with his twentieth-century Jesuit sidekick, Bernard J. F. Lonergan.

For a cleric of the thirteenth century, Aquinas surprised me by considering points of views contrary to his own and addressing them with concise answers. But above all, I found his position on conscience a show-stopper. He argued in defense of a heretic, a Christian who maintains a belief contrary to Church dogma. He maintained that the heretic would be committing a mortal sin, the hell-damning kind, by acquiescing to the Church's demand for conformity in violation of his own conscience. I was amazed that Aquinas, over 600 years before, had supported holding on to one's beliefs, the ones carefully considered and not whimsical, against the strong teachings of the Church. I inhaled the fresh air of openness Aquinas and Lonergan let in. For me their words stamped approval on asking questions regardless of where they led, a freedom that tugged on the door of my quarantine.

Like Aquinas, Bernard Lonergan, whose devotees affectionately called him "Bernie," spent a great deal of time writing philosophy. Lonergan's book *Insight: A Study of Human Understanding* had preceded my arrival at the Mount and had stirred up controversy. Lonergan purportedly wrote the book because he believed the philosophy currently being taught was not up to the job of supporting his theological thinking, like a Volkswagen frame not being adequate for the engine, cab, and cargo of a Mack truck.

The traditional philosophers on the faculty didn't take kindly to Lonergan's modern ideas. Subtle tensions had developed within the faculty, a fault line I had never seen before in the Order. My fellow philosophers and I took up positions in one of two main camps: "He's a twentieth century Aquinas breaking new ground" or "He strays too far from what we already know." I formed an allegiance with the first, but realized that I didn't understand his thought to the depth I wanted.

I liked Lonergan's directness, which sometimes arrived with a bite. A few sentences into the Preface of *Insight,* he wrote, "It [insight] is not any recondite intuition but the familiar event that occurs easily and frequently in the moderately intelligent, rarely and with difficulty only in the very stupid." And with that opening he wrote over seven hundred pages weaving a tapestry with threads from the scientific method, statistics, physics, common sense, and ethics.

More than anyone else, Lonergan provided a solid foundation on which I began to see the world differently. He convinced me that everyone possessed a God-given drive, "a pure desire to know." That drive pushed Galileo to peer through his telescope and Archimedes in his bathtub to problem-solve the displacement of water. I grew convinced that the desire to know was the engine propelling curiosity, philosophy, science, and probably religion.

Lonergan's pure desire-to-know legitimized, as Aquinas's position on conscience had, my itch to question. Like Michelangelo, lying on his back atop scaffolding and painting the ceiling of the Sistine Chapel, Lonergan was painting a philosophy unafraid of science, mathematics, or wherever inquiry led. Grasping his clear but dense prose combined agony and ecstasy. I read, reread, and mulled over his words. At times, I experienced a high in grasping one of his concepts. Reading Lonergan made me wonder how much it compared with the struggle to summit Mount Rainer for the view.

I began to see the desire to know as a force that created questions in every facet of life: physicists ask, "Why is gravity such a weak force?"; philosophers ask, "What is justice?"; theologians ask, "Is the God of the Old Testament the God of the New Testament?" I saw Lonergan's desire to know as dissolving the taboo surrounding troublesome questions, and quarantined questions, which percolated in my life and about my life.

TREMORS

With the freedom I had exercised during vacation at Hayden Lake in reading Steinbeck's *Cannery Row*, I enjoyed reading books other than those in philosophy. For leisure reading, I checked out James Joyce's *A Portrait of the Artist as a Young Man*. After just a few pages, I felt as if I were riding beside Stephen Dedalus, Joyce's main character, on a spiritual roller coaster. As a teenager I too had become sexually active. We both had experienced the guilt induced by a three-day version of the Spiritual Exercises. We both had death blown into our souls. Joyce's words dragged me back to my retreat in high school, but his searing experience outdid the milder version I'd felt at his age. The Jesuit priest Joyce portrayed as focused on death and judgment matched the first week of my long retreat. What he felt, I had felt during the Novitiate's thirty-day retreat that branded me with Ignatian spirituality.

Caught up in the *Portrait*, I sat alone in my room reading when the schedule required that I be outside exercising. The parallels between Stephen and me seemed uncanny. He entered an ascetic period; I entered the Order. The sermon that terrorized Stephen and drove him into his ascetic period set my memory reverberating with similar words I'd listened to and had taken to heart: "Consider the innumerable others who have gone to hell for fewer sins; remember the grievousness and malice of sin against our Creator and Lord; consider how in sinning and acting against Infinite Goodness, one has justly been condemned forever." I felt an urge to say out loud, but not loud enough to be heard in the hall outside my door, "I've had the same terror."

Stephen turned his back on sins of the flesh and rebounded into piety; guilt led me to search for a spiritual solution. Stephen declined the invitation to enter the Order; I sought entry, finding it a perfect solution to my sinfulness and a

perfect answer to my serving the Church in the highest calling I knew—the priesthood. We both had seen priests going
through the motions of the priesthood in a life that only had
a semblance of reality. Joyce outlined for me the downside risk
of Jesuit life in his depiction of the limping dean of studies as
a loveless shell of a man in whom the fire of Ignatian spirituality had gone out. I feared the same fate were I to lack the firm
footing of commitment. Unlike me, Stephen opted not to enter
the Order and charted his own course, leaving Ireland after
graduation to pursue his writing career in France. I continued
to maintain my Jesuit course.

Meeting Stephen shook my Jesuit life and my faith. *Will
spirituality become as elusive as metaphysics? Is the spirituality I know
an illusion? Will I become a priest just following rituals?* These questions reopened the initial dark days of the Juniorate and co-
agulated into fresh doubts.

Over the following months I gradually saw the quarantine
in a different light. It was as if I'd found a secret room in a
home I'd lived in for years. The absence of a spiritual director
I could relate to, the mixture of silence and solitude, and the
prohibition against sharing with peers led me to begin picking
the lock on my quarantine. I didn't do it regularly or systemati-
cally. It was hit-and-miss. During the introductory psychology
course we all took, I realized how little I was aware of emotions.
I began to recognize anger and how guilt camped in my daily
living. Only gradually did I begin to cobble together a syntax
of emotions that began with my experiencing the relentless
quest that Joyce had breathed into Stephen Daedalus. Much of
the time, my awareness of feelings was hazy, muted, and seen
through a glass darkly.

When my thoughts and feelings overheated with too many
questions about the religious life, I steadied myself with the
time-tested *Age quod agis—Do what you are doing.* Studying

philosophy and journeying on helped me reinstate the quarantine around the doubting part of me infected by questioning. Two steps forward, one step back. Or was it the reverse?

DARK COMEDY

Surrounded with witty, smart, and sometimes irreverent peers, the comic relief I found in day-to-day events was an antidote for my darker moments. The Mount was home not only to Jesuits in training but to deceased Jesuits of the Oregon Province. The Jesuit cemetery stood a few feet off the last turn on the twisting road leading to the seminary building. Like the Mount, the cemetery sat on volcanic basalt rock. A new death mobilized philosophers on the burial crew who would begin digging through the top soil at the assigned plot. Inevitably, after a few feet of easy digging, the clang of shovel on rock would signal the need for the jackhammer and its wheeled compressor. It often took more than a few days to break up the rock and reach the proper depth.

The death of an Oregon Jesuit occasionally took a comic turn. The prepared grave often stood open for a few days awaiting its occupant. More than once a meandering skunk, armed with curiosity and poor judgment, would find itself at the bottom of the open grave. Unable to get out, the skunk would put up a stink that called for the return of the burial crew. Each rescue stood as an ironic reminder to us Oregon Jesuits that we would end up here, but without a crew to rescue us.

THE CHALLENGE OF ZOOLOGY

After completing the pre-med chemistry requirements, I enrolled in *Vertebrate Zoology* and its accompanying lab course during the second semester of my second year at the Mount.

Following the professor's final exam, I had only the lab final to wind up the course. The lab assistant, an attractive coed finishing her biology major, had overseen our dissection of worms, frogs, and the main attraction—a fetal pig. Her quiz required students, one-by-one, to move to each of twenty stations. The first nineteen held trays with parts of a dissected pig skewered with colorful numbered pins. Armed with our memory and a test paper, each of us was given a thirty-second stop to write down the name of the pinned organ. At the last station, which was set apart for a five-item oral quiz, the lab assistant stood in her white lab coat. For me, the only student wearing a cassock, she limited her oral exam to one area of the pig's anatomy.

Using her tweezers, she pointed or picked up what she wanted me to identify.

"What is this?"

"Seminiferous tubule."

"And this?"

"The vas deferens."

"And this?"

"The scrotal sac."

"And this?"

"A testis."

"And this?"

"A penis."

I never learned why in my case this coed focused her quiz on the genital system. Perhaps she was just having fun. When I reflected on the incident, I awakened to the fact that chastity had never felt bothersome. Perhaps my guilt over sex with Maureen had neutered me. Since entering the Order I'd never masturbated or had a need to. I passed over any sexual scenes in the few movies I'd seen much like glancing at a billboard while driving by. I hoped the vow of chastity had tranquilized

my sexuality like Ron's Xylocaine injections deadened a bothersome tooth.

A Change of Course

With end of the school year, the dean of studies arrived for our
annual meeting.

"Mr. Tracy, I see you have earned very good grades in each
of your science courses," he began. "Have you taken any additional psychology courses other than the introductory one
everyone takes in the first year?"

"That's the only one I've taken," I said.

"The reason I ask is that we've decided that the Province's
needs are better met with your pursuing a postgraduate degree
in psychology rather than continuing toward psychiatry."

My gaze slipped from his face to a small stain on the lapel
of his suitcoat. I felt my breathing stop. I wasn't holding my
breath. It was a quiet pause, as if a motor had stopped somewhere inside me. Then, breathing started again.

"I think it would be good for you to begin this summer ac-
cumulating courses for a major in psychology."

I managed a slow affirmative nod of my head, a downward
glance, and a neutral, "That sounds fine."

Like our brief meeting two years before, this one ended in
less than five minutes. Over the next few days, I was less talkative
at recreation times. I started getting my bearings by finding the
Gonzaga summer school catalogue and looking over the upcom-
ing offerings in psychology. In fact, the course in personality dy-
namics pulled me into the field of motivation and the myriad
factors that propel our choices. Statistics, the other course I
took, analyzed data no less scientifically than the beakers and
test tubes I had used the previous summer. By the end of summer, I had begun adjusting to the unexpected change of course.

PHILOSOPHY AND PSYCHOLOGY

The packed schedule of the third and last year of philosophy carried me toward completion of my stay at the Mount. There were six graduate courses in philosophy, upper-level under-graduate courses in psychology on the Gonzaga campus, and a final thesis in philosophy—eighteen hours the first semester, twenty-two hours the second, which included eight hours of student teaching. Hypomania was the order of the day. The whirlwind mixture of philosophy and psychology had stirred my interest in writing a thesis that focused on moral judgment. I set about weaving together the views of Thomas Aquinas and psychologist Jean Piaget. As best as I could, I let the desire-to-know form the questions to be answered in my thesis.

Clearly, Aquinas's notion of a person's conscience challenging authority had never left me. I read developmental psychology in hopes of finding the roots of conscience. I found Jean Piaget, a Swiss psychologist, who had explored conscience and morality. He outlined a framework based on watching children at play. From his observations he came to believe that the way children observe or break the rules in games foreshadows the moral tension between the dictates of authority and the judgment of the individual.

In an unused storage room next to the makeshift living quarters I'd slept in and sweated in, during my first summer at the Mount, I found an eight-foot Army blanket mounted upright on a frame that helped subdivide the room for a now-unknown purpose. It was the perfect place to sort through my references, dutifully recorded on three-by-five cards. There, armed with a box of straight pins and my note cards, I began pinning them across almost fifty square feet of wool. I struggled to put together ethics and psychology. Like an artist with his paintbrush, I'd step back and eye the arrangement, adding new cards from ongoing research, shifting clusters to a new area, and removing cards that didn't advance my reasoning. Here I'd come each evening to review the blanket of ideas before my final visit to the chapel.

During the second semester, a night course in counseling at Gonzaga paralleled my thesis writing. Father Evoy, a silver-haired Jesuit psychologist on the faculty, radiated contagious optimism. His upbeat voice, smile, and the sparkle in his eyes subtracted years from his fifty-something age. He brought to mind the young scholastics at Seattle Prep like Mr. Reilly and Mr. Galbraith, whose personalities had drawn my admiration. Now this Jesuit priest-psychologist modeled and taught me the basics of "Client-Centered" therapy that psychologist Carl Rogers had developed.

The theory underpinning the therapy maintained that individuals possess the potential, under the proper conditions, to develop and restructure themselves. The proper conditions included low threat and an empathic counselor who listens well and mirrors accurately what the person was saying. Interpreting what the person said, making judgments about it, or telling a person what to do—all these did not fit with non-directive counseling principles. I was drawn to this psychology, which believed in the growth potential of the individual.

The course brought a pleasant breeze of openness flowing counter to the strong winds of authority, not only the authority of a directive counselor but also the authority that Piaget had written about and I had experienced. After my second class with Father Evoy and the bus ride back to the Mount, I took the stairs two at a time to the blanket, books, and notes waiting for me on the third-floor. I found the passage where Piaget, Aquinas, and Rogers intersected: "...among these [social] relations we can distinguish two extreme types: **relations of constraint**, whose characteristic is to impose upon the individual from outside a system of rules with obligatory content, and **relations of cooperation,** whose characteristic is to create within people's minds the consciousness of ideal norms at the back of all rules [emphasis added]." I stayed awake until midnight weaving together the threads that would form the final pattern of my thesis, a pattern that addressed my growing need for freedom as the connection between ethics and psychology.

The satisfaction of completing the thesis, which marked the end of philosophy studies, brought with it a reminder that I was on a road leading to ordination as a Catholic priest. Yet even well-educated Catholics often don't know that ordination as a full-fledged priest takes seven steps, called "orders." The completion of my studies at the Mount would bring ordination in the first four "minor orders"—acolyte, exorcist, reader, and porter. *Exorcist?* I had read little about exorcism and had given no serious thought to the process of driving Satan out of a possessed person. Neither had I given much thought to Satan, the fallen archangel depicted as roaming the world trying to seduce us mortals into sins deserving of his home in hell.

During an ecumenical dinner a Spokane rabbi hosted for a few of us third-year philosophers, one of my companions made a passing comment about our approaching ordination as exorcists. "You believe in "dybbuks?" he exclaimed in disbelief. My wrinkled, quizzical expression likely prompted him to explain that in his tradition dybbuks were evil spirits of dislocated souls that attached themselves to living people. His reaction turned the crank of questioning within me. *Was the ritual of exorcising devils a sincere, but misguided, attempt to deal with a wide range of abnormal or unusual behaviors that modern medicine could examine and diagnose if diagnosis was called for?* But this question was a tremor not as strong as the quake James Joyce had triggered earlier. I reflexively quarantined it. My quarantine had grown more subtle, often masquerading as procrastination—*I'll deal with it later.*

MOVING ON

In leaving the Mount, I completed a stormy voyage with a Jesuit crew knitted together over the past three years, but now dispersing. Most of the Canadians I'd likely not see again because they would study theology back home; many Californians I'd probably see in three years for theological studies in California; others would be off to theology studies in Europe. And undoubtedly some would leave the Order for parts unknown. Like the metamorphosis of amphibians I had studied in biology with their growth, differentiation, and programmed cell death, the Order was evolving—developing, differentiating, and letting go of members no longer suited for the mission. A shadow of sadness passed over me before I looked toward the sunshine of moving forward. I had finished the third leg of the journey to the priesthood—Novitiate, Juniorate, and now philosophy, with regency and theology ahead.

The Order's routine of regency meant almost all of us would teach high school. My first step into experiencing the "real" world as a Jesuit teacher beckoned. Student teaching during the final semester had let me escape, at least for six weeks, from the hothouse of studies. I had observed competent teachers. I had created my own lesson plans. I had taught classes. I had received the respect given members of the faculty. I had felt a surge in reconnecting with the world outside a seminary.

The Province dean's review of my transcript led him to conclude that I was qualified to teach English, Latin, or chemistry, or some combination of the three. Based on that assessment and the teaching needs of the four high schools in the Province, I was assigned to begin teaching in the fall at Bellarmine Prep in Tacoma.

I left the Mount enriched most by the philosophy of Lonergan and the psychology of Carl Rogers. I also left increasingly aware that the Order gloved the hand of the Church that had been molding me as long as I could remember. While eager to move forward, I knew I'd face unexpected challenges.

CHAPTER 9

Regency

I left Mount St. Michael in June 1963 for Seattle University. Seattle U offered me more courses to fill out a psychology major. Along with several Jesuits, I joined regular students living in Bellarmine Hall. At first, the shift from the quiet of Mount St. Michael, surrounded by farmland, to the buzz of dormitory exchanges thirty feet from traffic whizzing by on 12th Avenue bewildered me. Dormitory living brought open group showers like I'd taken in high school athletics, a big change from the curtained shower of the seminary. At Seattle U, we took our meals in the cafeteria with other summer school students. The blend of Jesuits with non-Jesuit students brought mealtime conversation. I liked the many changes.

Registering for classes was an adventure I'd never faced before. I read the how-to instructions three times, then worked my way through the lines to sign up for classes. I came out of the registrar's office to find a scholastic huddled on the floor against the opposite wall. His hands shook. His voice quavered, "I can't do it." It took two of us to get him registered—I was able to get him to tell me what classes he wanted to take, the other scholastic filled out the forms. I knew this classmate as insecure and lacking confidence. I think he unraveled under the pressure of acting on his own, a foreign, sometimes forbidden, act within the walls of seminary living.

An upside summer school benefit for me was the easily granted permission to visit my parents who lived just twenty minutes away. My folks had never visited Mount St. Michael as they had Sheridan. Letters kept us in touch. I had tracked Mom's success in her Bellevue business and Dad's steady march toward retirement. He would reach sixty-five in November. During my first Sunday dinner at home, Dad told me he would continue working until Mom chose to sell her half of the knitting business. I saw how Dad's hair was edging from gray to white and how Mom was losing speed in her steady step. Ron had finished his stint in the Army and started a dental practice in a Seattle suburb. He and his wife had welcomed their third child less than a month before.

Ron beamed with pride in showing off his children. And his enthusiasm for dentistry bubbled to the surface right away. He took me aside and asked, "Do you still have your wisdom teeth?"

"Of course," I said, "I've brushed my teeth well and have never had a toothache needing a dentist."

"Open your mouth real wide."

After a minute of tilting my head from side to side and peering intently, he said, "Those wisdom teeth need to come out. Keeping them any longer is not a good idea. Call the office and make an appointment."

His question reminded me how lucky I was never to have needed a physical or dental exam since entering the Order.

BELLARMINE PREP

Summer school beefed up my transcript for hoped-for graduate school after ordination. What preoccupied me more than summer courses were the unknown classes I'd teach at Bellarmine

High. Would I be teaching chemistry, English, Latin, or a mix? The question kept distracting me during morning meditations.

In late July, Father Williams, the new principal at Bellarmine, sent me a hand-scrawled note, "Mr. Tracy, you will be teaching junior Latin and the three classes of junior English. The book ordering schedule is tight so you'll need to review textbooks we have on hand and give me recommendations for replacements or for supplementary texts." I was relieved at not teaching chemistry. I eagerly searched for new textbooks, especially for junior English.

With the end of my summer studies, I arrived at the Bellarmine High School campus on a sweltering August afternoon. I scanned the buildings, ringed around a parking lot half the size of a football field—the red brick Jesuit residence, the new cream-colored gymnasium, and the school wrapped in brick identical to the Jesuit living quarters. I prepared to do God's work as a high school teacher for the next few years.

After supper, I met Father Williams face-to-face for the first time. He was a first-year principal who didn't fit the authoritarian profile of a Jesuit principal like Father McDonnell, who'd kept me and my friends in line at Seattle Prep. Flecks of white salted his black hair. His voice flowed in a soft, measured way. Before he entered the Jesuits, he was part of the World War II American occupation forces in Japan. Perhaps Jesuit decision-makers found his military background good training for his new assignment of managing an all-boys high school.

Only at the end of our brief chat did he add nonchalantly, "By the way, you'll be coaching football, basketball, and track." Those assignments were scary and stimulating. I knew the most about football, less about basketball, and almost nothing about track. The upside was that Father Williams assumed I could meet those demands.

Mid-month, just after Ron had extracted all four of my wisdom teeth, I sat down with two other assistant coaches and the first-year football coach. The new coach was blond, young, and eager to have us learn his system and prepare for twice-a-day practices, which began before the start of school. At the first practice I walked rather than ran and avoided demonstrating blocks because exertion increased the pain in my jaw. Although it took a week for me to rev up the gung-ho rhythm of a credible football coach, nothing dampened my eagerness to be what Ignatius had called "a contemplative in action."

SETTLING IN

We regents did have relaxing breaks. Bellarmine's small Jesuit community (eleven priests and eight non-priests) contrasted sharply with the Mount Saint Michael community of more than a hundred. After football practice, class preparation, and supper, I plopped into the sofa next to George Dahlquist. I welcomed the freedom for us scholastics to call each other by our first names, not, of course, in front of students. George and I had moved as companions through each phase of the Order, including chemistry courses at the Mount.

All of us scholastics watched the blockbuster evening news of August 28, 1963. My eyes locked on the replay of Martin Luther King's "I Have a Dream" speech before the 250,000 who had marched with him to Washington, D.C. The freedom to hear world news, prohibited in the Novitiate and Juniorate, had arrived. For me, it was better than the eventual freedom to eat meat on Fridays.

During the final week run-up to the September school opening, I was startled to see a new face at the priests' dinner table. Last-minute teaching assignments were not uncommon for priests. I recognized the face—Father Coughlin ("Father

Fingers"). The memory of his tutoring me in freshman Latin eleven years before broke out of my quarantine. The next day, I checked his class assignments—sophomore Latin. *Better than freshman Latin.* Although I don't recall avoiding Father Coughlin, he and I never exchanged a word. Whenever I saw him talking to a student, a yellow light went on inside me. I always noted where his hands were. Never seeing anything remarkable, I quarantined my concern.

I veered away from the Jesuit routine I'd followed for the previous seven years. Rather than being a year-round student facing a teacher, now I was the teacher facing students. When I walked into class the first week, my energy was full throttle, as if I'd just downed three cups of coffee.

TEACHING

From the outset, intuition guided my teaching of English. I wanted to balance structure and freedom. I had never accepted a belief peddled in one education class. The instructor claimed if young children were given complete freedom to choose whatever they wanted to eat, they'd end up selecting a nutritious diet. Unbelievable nonsense! I aimed to teach how to structure an essay, tighten a paragraph, and expand vocabulary. Those elements were the meat and potatoes of writing. Fancy desserts could come later, in college.

Bellarmine High School Faculty Member, 1965

On the side of freedom, I took Rogers' method of student-centered teaching into the classroom. Twice a week, I launched class discussions on the assigned reading with simple questions like, "In *Self-Reliance,* what do you think Emerson is driving at?" I'd paraphrase the boys' comments and not interject my opinion. I marveled how in forty-five minutes these third-year high school students generated more clarity and insight into what they had read than I could have bored them with in a prepared lecture. With paraphrasing prompts, juniors sifted insights from the essays of Henry Thoreau and the poetry of Robert Frost. Carl Rogers' power in the classroom was amazing. Although I required book reports, students were completely free to choose what to read. The range they chose stretched from *PT 109* to *One Day in the Life of Ivan Denisovich.* Gradually, I recognized the structure and freedom I delivered in teaching reflected my desire for both.

During the first semester, a bright regent who was a year ahead invited me to join him in foraging for books at the Tacoma Public Library. After supper every other Thursday, we drove downtown to the library's main branch to look over new acquisitions and check out books for class preparation and leisure reading. During my first visit, I followed the freedom of choice I was preaching in English class. I had never forgotten Ron's sending me Jack Kerouac's *On the Road* in the Juniorate, its removal, and the suspicious cross-examination I'd undergone. I found it and checked it out. Kerouac's writing style intrigued me. It throbbed with a rhythm I'd felt when reading Joyce's *Portrait of an Artist.* It helped me pause and breathe in the fresh air of choices I now made—although not even close to the wild and drunken ones Kerouac had made.

Because I didn't teach a class during third period, the principal assigned me the job of typing up announcements for the day and distributing them to each classroom by the end of the period. The job challenged me to avoid typing mistakes on ditto-masters, which couldn't be easily corrected. Then I had to run off the dittoes fast enough to avoid the headache that came from inhaling the volatile fluid evaporating off moist copies.

On Friday, November 22, 1963, as I was rolling the ditto master into the typewriter Father Williams came into the faculty room and turned on the radio. The announcer said, "President Kennedy has been shot in Dallas, Texas." The words froze the four of us in the room. I started typing the news only after the fateful report came in from Parkland Hospital. As I distributed the news of President Kennedy's assassination, the principal announced over the intercom that an optional noon Mass would be said for our slain president. The chapel filled to standing-room only. The Mass provided solace to stunned students and faculty, and backlit the comforting role of the Church in times of crisis. During meditation the next morning, I prayed for the strength to serve the Church as a priest-psychologist comforting others.

COACHING

As frosh basketball coach, I took Rogers' psychology to the basketball court. I was faced with sending a ninth-grade squad into a tenth-grade league made up of large public schools, all of them with male students some multiple of the number at Bellarmine. The superior size, strength, and experience of fifteen-year-olds versus fourteen-year-olds can never be missed. Fortunately, the twelve Bellarmine freshmen players I had selected during tryouts included gifted athletes. I ran all twelve through drills of dribbling with each hand, making outlet passes, getting the ball to the open man, and controlling the tempo of play.

In the first game of the season, after we had quickly fallen behind, I called a time-out.

"What's happening out there?" I asked.

"We're bunching up and not spreading the floor," said one.

"What else?"

"We're not hitting the open man," added another.

"What else?"

"We're not making the outlet pass fast enough after re-bounds," said a third.

"So you know what you need to do."

Then the ninth-graders battled back and by the second half had taken the lead on their way to winning. They won sixteen of eighteen games and took second place in the league. I sensed Carl Rogers sitting beside me on the bench during each of those games.

RELAXING

It was hard to blend the demands of teaching and coaching with the routine spiritual rhythms that remained the same—an hour of morning meditation, Mass, and two daily examinations of conscience. I had never guessed how fast the tempo would be.

Occasionally, a small group of us regents would coax a young priest to join us for a weekend outing to a cottage Bellarmine owned at Gig Harbor. The small, white-frame getaway sat less than thirty feet from the shore at high tide. Roof-sloped rooms above the main floor served as sleeping quarters. An alcove on the main floor became a makeshift chapel where our priest-in-residence would say morning Mass after meditation. We corrected papers or read in the living room with its view of small boats anchored off shore. We even enjoyed a few drinks before making supper. Those getaways taught me that modern contemplatives could consume moderate amounts of McNaughton's blended whiskey while doing God's work.

Wherever we were, lighthearted joking and banter (always respectful) continued to ebb and flow between us regents. We carefully observed the unwritten code of never prying into a fellow Jesuit's thoughts or feelings, and never disclosed personal misgivings about the life we were living. I don't recall ever sharing a raw emotion or dreams about the future. My demanding schedule crowded out wide-ranging reflection. The fast pace of living substituted for the quarantine I'd used to keep safe my faith and way of life. I maintained my march under the Jesuit banner "For the Greater Glory of God" within the narrow boundaries of meditation and ongoing critical self-examination.

SPIRITUAL GUIDE

The students taught me that teenagers in the mid-60s were not much different from me and my high school classmates in the mid-50s. We shared Catholicism, girls, and the search for role models. I felt awkward knowing some students put me and my way of life on a pedestal as I had done with Jesuits I had admired in high school. Now, living the Jesuit life, I knew I was not different from other men. I recalled my father's wisdom—"All men put their pants on one leg at a time."

The fact that I'd played sports in high school and now was coaching at Bellarmine probably influenced several athletes to join the Sodality, which I moderated. The Sodality, short for *The Sodality of the Virgin Mary*, brought Catholic students together to do more than just go to Mass on Sunday. Following Sodality goals, I shepherded them into extra Catholic activities, like getting involved in charitable work. St. Matthew's gospel listed the good works Christ had spoken of, like visiting the sick. The scripture gave me the idea of scheduling regular visits to a Tacoma home for the elderly.

No amount of pleasant talk following "Hi, I'm Vern, a student from Bellarmine" could spark a connection with a senior citizen ravaged by dementia. Slow responses, unrelated to a student's query, mixed with the pervasive scent of pine oil cleaner, which didn't mask the underlying odor of urine, extinguished the students' fire for this form of Christian charity. I felt guilty about frustrating the students and disappointing the elderly. However, I recognized a failing experiment when I saw it. I accepted the fact of blind alleys blocking the pursuit of lofty causes. I regrouped and searched for good works that fit better with teenage Catholic boys.

SUMMER 1964

At the end of the school year, I returned to Seattle University for another summer of psychology courses. The return brought a reunion with several Novitiate classmates who'd entered the Order with me. At least ten in our class were attending summer school at other universities. Others had left the Society. No conversations speculated on the reason Gary or Nick had left. Those of us who remained journeyed on. In the evenings we swapped stories of embarrassing moments in the classroom or ribbed each other about rivalries between the schools where we taught, like Seattle Prep versus Bellarmine. The banter continued to weave our individual journeys into the fabric of the Order.

After summer school, seven of us regents and one priest from Bellarmine were treated to a one-week break at a benefactor's vacation home on Warm Beach. The gray, weather-stained bungalow sat on a bluff overlooking the inland waters of Puget Sound. Balmy, westerly salt-scented breezes swept up the thirty-foot embankment and through the open windows. The tide lapped in and out twice a day over a sandy bar. In August, Mother Nature showed me a sight I'd never seen before.

After meditation the second morning, I walked alone on the beach at low tide. I came across pools up to four-feet deep and thirty-feet long. A silvery flash caught my attention. Looking closer I saw several salmon had become trapped. I had to join them. I took off my shoes and waded in. The suction of wet sand mixed with mud brought me to a stop in water just below my waist. The sun had raised the temperature of the water making it pleasant compared to the usually frigid waters of the Sound. Three-to-four-foot salmon bulleted around me. I began to dance with the fish. I pumped my feet up and down on the sticky bottom. The shimmering salmon would slingshot between my legs or brush against one. I dropped my hands to the same depth as an approaching fish. Several times, I managed to grab and hold a salmon for a few seconds before its wiggle and slippery skin freed it from my grasp. My dance with the salmon went on for several minutes until I stopped, exhausted.

I resumed my walk along the beach, waiting for my pants to dry and to make sense out of what had just happened. A calm much deeper than I'd experienced during any meditation came over me. I recalled the passage in St. Matthew's gospel where Jesus came across Peter and Andrew fishing in the Sea of Galilee. He recruited them as disciples by simply saying, "Follow me, and I will make you fishers of men." *Had my dance with the fish been a spiritual encounter?* I wondered whether the salmon's easy escape from my grip was warning me that becoming a fisher of men would not be easy.

The next morning, when I hurried down to the beach, the salmon were gone and ribbed sand had replaced the pools.

REGENCY, YEAR 2

I returned refreshed to Bellarmine in late August to begin my second year of regency. The worry that comes with being a first-year teacher was gone. Father Coughlin was gone. A freshman English class replaced my third-year Latin class. Now, with four English classes to teach, I winced at the thought of more compositions to correct. Still, I looked forward to teaching bright fourteen-year-olds just entering high school.

The discouraging scores on the football field that season were not as disheartening as the news from Vatican II, the ecumenical council opened by Pope John XXIII in 1962. My hopes for significant Church reform had dimmed with Pope John's death in June of 1963. Now, in late October 1964, at the beginning of the second session of the council, I read the newspaper report of Cardinal Suenens goading his peers and giving hope to women with the question, "Why are we even discussing the reality of the Church when half of the Church is not even represented here?" My hopes for major church reforms dimmed.

October did bring a bright spot. Discussions at home and a barrage of TV ads about the approaching presidential election amped up the political interest of most of the juniors. In 1964, the Republicans chose Barry Goldwater to carry the conservative banner against President Lyndon Johnson, who had become president following the assassination of President Kennedy. I saw an opening. The junior English classes overwhelmingly favored Johnson. I suspected most students mirrored their parents' choice. I knew my cassock and role as teacher could easily sway their opinions. After all, they were impressionable sixteen-year-olds. I resolved to see whether a non-directive approach could foster more respect between the Democratic majority and the few beleaguered Republicans.

"Mark, you see Goldwater as following the Constitution more closely than the president."

"Ed, you find Johnson's position on discrimination as closer to the Church's teaching on justice."

In spite of my attempts to keep the class focused on hearing what "each side" was saying, both sides worked their way back to me. They knew I would be voting.

"Mr. Tracy, what do you think?"

"Whose position do you think is right?"

After the election I took a vote on whom they believed I voted for. The Democratic students were convinced I had voted for Johnson; the Republican students all believed I had voted for Goldwater. I came away satisfied I'd not stepped in with obvious or subtle pressure. In spite of student badgering, I never disclosed my vote.

MEETING ALBERT

During a December outing to the Tacoma library, I meandered to the philosophy section where Albert Camus' *The Myth of Sisyphus* caught my eye. During philosophy I hadn't read any of his books or essays but did recall a controversy about whether or not he was a "real" existentialist philosopher. Flipping to the first sentence of the book, I read, "There is but one truly serious philosophical problem, and that is suicide. Judging whether life is or is not worth living amounts to answering the fundamental question of philosophy." The sledgehammer directness made me check out the book.

As I squeezed in bursts of reading Camus between teaching and coaching, I came across his notion of "absurdity." He believed life has no meaning delivered by God or religion or any source outside us, and does not necessarily lead to suicide. Rather, he believed we need to create and put meaning into our lives without the payoff of a life hereafter. For him, nobility in life flows from defiantly facing life's absurdity, the irreconcilable conflicts in one's life.

While I maintained my commitment to the Jesuit ideal of serving others under the banner of Christ, I realized I was running on automatic pilot. And I had to admit to myself I fell short of Camus' standard. I fueled my endurance as a Jesuit with the belief that God would reward me in the next life. I wrestled with Camus' ideas and came away feeling tired and overmatched, but also feeling much of what he wrote made sense. Yet, I didn't feel the disorienting tremors I had experienced at the Mount when I encountered *Portrait of an Artist*. I told myself I was too busy to sort through Camus' challenges while, at a deeper level, I was slipping them into quarantine.

JUMP AHEAD

In the early spring of 1965, Father Kaufman, the Province dean of studies who had started and stopped my pre-med studies, arrived for another of his yearly visits. Assuming I'd be returning to Seattle University for a summer of more psychology courses, I thought my meeting would be short and routine.

"Father Royce at Seattle U has made a suggestion," he began.

I knew Father Royce from a distance. He was chairman of the psychology department at SU. I'd only spoken with him a few times during the previous two summer schools.

"He's suggested you be sent to theology a year early."

"You mean I wouldn't be returning to Bellarmine for a third year of teaching?" I said.

"Yes. The provincial has approved the plan, so you'll be moving on to Alma College in California in June for the start of theological studies."

My breathing halted; I felt my heart beating. I restarted my breathing as if I'd just broken the surface after a deep dive.

"Really?" was all I could muster.

And with a few forgotten concluding words, Father Kaufman ended our brief meeting.

I knew many who entered the Order in their thirties or forties or who arrived with college degrees often were pushed ahead. I certainly didn't fit those groups. Whatever the reason, I'd reach theology and the priesthood ahead of schedule.

Walking down the hall, I sensed my body was pleasantly unhinged as if my feet and arms were disjointed, like a puppet on a string. The bodily sense stayed with me as I left the faculty house for a walk on the track around the football field. As I walked I scrolled through events of the two years of regency with its teaching, coaching, and living a Jesuit life different from the prior seven years. I had whisked along on a speed train from which I only caught glimpses of a country and world embroiled in change—Kennedy's assassination, the Hippies, the Beatles, President Johnson's "Great Society," and the first U.S. combat troops in Vietnam. I had worked hard day-to-day for two years with only a snapshot awareness of the changes taking place in the world and inside me.

Over the next few days, I shared the news with the third-year regents slated for theology—two in Toronto, one other in California, where I'd be going. Of course, I also told George Dahlquist, who was happy for me although it was a break in our tandem moves in the Order. He had another year of regency. I again recalled how newly ordained priests stopped at Sheridan to encourage us novices. All had described the four years of theology as the pinnacle of Jesuit education towering above the classics and philosophy. Theology and the priesthood would come bundled together. I expected the combination would bring me closer to God, whom I had been chasing since the days of rheumatic fever.

CHAPTER 10

First Year Theology

St. Ignatius High School in San Francisco was the overnight stopover on the way to theology studies. The other Bellarmine regent and I left Bellarmine and flew down on a June Friday to join other Oregon Jesuits and a few Californians for the final leg to Alma College, the Jesuit theological seminary in California. Jack, a native San Franciscan, who had just completed three years teaching at his alma mater, St. Ignatius High School, suggested we pool whatever leftover travel money we had and go to dinner on Fisherman's Wharf.

We arrived in the early evening at an upscale restaurant on the wharf. Jack led the twelve of us, decked out in our clerical suits, through a packed waiting line toward a harried hostess. As Jack drew close to the hostess, the maître'd came forward and said, "Father, right this way," and proceeded to lead us past glum-faced patrons who likely had been waiting for some time. Two tables were quickly joined together to accommodate us or the twelve apostles.

Sitting next to Jack I asked, "Did you make reservations?"

"No," he quietly replied.

"Do you know someone here?"

"No."

"How did we get preference?"

"Clerical privilege."

I winced and vainly searched the menu for something my contribution to our money pool would cover.

Clerical privilege continued to unfold. Caesar salad and Chilean sea bass followed my gin and tonic and was joined by a glass of California chardonnay. Dessert and coffee reawakened my slumbering concern about our ability to pay for the dinner.

The waiter came and whispered in Jack's ear. Jack rose and walked to a table about twenty feet away where a party of six was dining. He talked briefly and smilingly to a gray-haired gentleman who had stood and shook his hand. When he returned Jack said the man had picked up the tab for our entire group.

"Why," I asked.

"He's the father of a student I taught at St. Ignatius. Although his son isn't a strong student, I did write a positive letter to Santa Clara that probably helped him get accepted. His dad said our dinners are just part of his business expense."

My gratitude arm-wrestled with my embarrassment in the face of this additional clerical privilege.

ALMA COLLEGE

The next morning, we loaded our luggage and ourselves into two VW vans for the ride to Alma, our home for the next four years. Driving south from San Francisco on the 280 Freeway, we branched onto the West Valley Freeway, which took us away from the densely packed homes of the Bay area. A breeze through my partially opened window brought fresh morning air that was a welcome change from the foggy city air of San Francisco. We turned south onto Highway 17, which led us quickly through Los Gatos and then up the steepening incline of the Santa Cruz Mountains. The tall palm trees that had lined the streets of Los Gatos gave way to the evergreens like those in the Northwest. Within a few minutes we turned off the highway and headed up a gravel road to the garages on the backside of Alma College. Those of us in the second van opted to walk the grounds before searching out our assigned rooms and dropping off our luggage.

Not far from where we parked, ten-foot cedar columns stood like sentinels spaced at intervals around a fifty-foot-long swimming pool. Cedar beams reached across the fifteen-foot-wide pool to join the wood pillars. If the wood had been marble, I would have thought we'd arrived at an outdoor Roman bath for the Caesars.

Father McShane, a Church historian famous among young Jesuits for his iconoclastic exposure of bogus saints, rose from his towel to greet us. His almond-tanned skin testified to hours around the pool and highlighted perfect white teeth in the midst of his smile.

"Welcome to Alma," he said.

We made the handshake-round of introducing ourselves before Father McShane told us we were in time for lunch. I walked around to the front entrance of the main building. There before me unrolled an emerald lawn that flowed downhill over a hundred yards, with low single-story classrooms on the left and three-story living quarters on the right. These buildings framed a small lake, where water from a center fountain geysered over thirty feet in the air. I stopped and inhaled the beauty of a scene artists would fight to paint. There couldn't be a more idyllic place to complete the final step in my journey to the priesthood.

The weekend provided time for us new theologians to settle into our rooms, eight-by-twelve affairs outfitted with bed, desk, and a sink. Fiberboard walls didn't offer much of a sound barrier to adjacent rooms, but did complement the cedar construction in all the buildings that made the entire complex a firebug's dream.

Alma College, Jesuit Theologate
(Jesuit Oregon Province Archives)

Reconnecting with California Jesuits who'd left Mount St. Michael for their teaching assignments, and with Oregon Jesuits who'd been scattered across the Northwest, enriched the bland potpourri of summer courses. Afternoon tennis or basketball kept us fit, while after-dinner bridge games clustered some of us into cagey good-natured bidding and bluffing. I felt the in-step rhythm with men I'd known for three to eight years, now reunited to continue the march toward a common goal. I marched in a Company of Jesuits. Life was good.

"You're going to love theology. It's the cherry on top of philosophy and the classics." That repeated refrain made me eager to march forward on the high road of theology.

THEOLOGY CLASSES

Monday brought summer school with five one-hour courses ranging from *Elementary Hebrew* to an *Introduction to the Old Testament*. Father O'Connor presented *Oriental Theology* in a fashion that struck me as organized according to the free associations of a psychoanalytic patient. He bounced us from the beauty of Byzantine triptych art to the gist of the preaching of St. John Chrysostom, archbishop of Constantinople. I used bubble note-taking, writing one idea within a circle with a line to the next circled idea, in an attempt to overcome confusion and dozing. I was able to pull together disjointed themes bubbled across my open notebook. This initiation into theology fell short of its billing.

Fall semester 1965 ushered in a first moral theology course, which I came to view as natural ethics supercharged with divine revelation. Boiled down, it was a practical course aimed at helping priests in the confessional sort out whether and to what degree a penitent's admissions fit sinfulness. My natural bent, reinforced by the influence of Carl Roger's non-directive counseling, ran counter to judging people's action. The mix of moral theology and psychology spelled trouble.

Father Joseph Farraher, a nationally known former editor of a prestigious periodical in moral theology, introduced us to the subject. His low-key modest demeanor made it hard to pick him out when he filed into the classroom with the rest of us. His stepping up to the lectern was often the first sign of his presence. Glasses and short-cropped hair complemented a neutral face that invited interpretation like a Rorschach card. The cadence of his voice gave a steady rhythm to the organized hand-written notes in front of him. His lecture style definitely contrasted with Father O'Connor's meandering summer course. Father Farraher's presentation kept me focused on his logic as he fitted one argument neatly to the next, like a craftsman laying out a parquet floor. When my gut tightened and signaled, *Something isn't right here,* I had a hard time finding a crooked seam in his reasoning.

To help guide us through the labyrinth of moral reasoning, a green four-by-six-inch volume summarizing solutions to moral problems written by a German priest, Heribert Jone, became our CliffsNotes in the course. This small book fit neatly in the hand and made me joke to some that perhaps a confessor's long pause behind the veiled grate of the confessional hid frantic paging to the right answer.

While looking through its pages, I braked to a stop on "covert compensation." In class, Father Farraher fleshed out the concept by explaining that greedy businessmen often increased the prices of goods in ghettoes because many local residents didn't have transportation to the lower-priced stores in more affluent areas.

Hence, a customer's covert pocketing of a few extras was compensation for being gouged. Economic justifications for higher item pricing, like increased overhead due to increased insurance rates associated with theft, were never discussed as a factor in higher pricing.

I asked, "Why not just say in plain English, 'Sometimes stealing is justified, like stealing bread to feed your hungry family'?" Father Farraher suggested we should avoid explaining the concept of covert compensation to the laity, aka non-clergy, because it could be easily misunderstood and then abused. I came away quietly unconvinced of the overall idea.

The topic of covert compensation qualified for the minor leagues compared to the major leagues of sexuality and birth control. In the case of a married couple having difficulties with conception, moral theology judged as sinful a husband providing, via masturbation, a sperm sample for testing. *Why?* The rote answer was: Because the act of masturbating is "intrinsically evil." I and others argued that because the ultimate aim of masturbation was procreation, it seemed appropriate and justified. Besides, to extract a sperm sample via an invasive medical procedure would be, to put it mildly, uncomfortable.

I countered by pointing out that chewing gum mobilized gastric juices that by nature were for digestion. Wouldn't natural law reasoning argue that chewing Wrigley's spearmint was a new form of masturbation? Such counter-arguments never blunted the dogmatic adherence to the intrinsic-evil argument.

The advent of "the pill" and its easy birth control the Church treated as a plague. The arguments favoring family planning via a pill rather than monthly roulette just wouldn't go away. Some Catholics, exercising thoughtful personal judgment, ignored the Church's prohibition while other couples could not overcome the Church's trump card of "intrinsic evil" or contrary to "natural law." Justifications like poverty, health, and personal choice were brushed aside like gnats.

In my reading, I came across an article that touched on the turmoil in the Belgian Congo that mentioned the raping of nuns. One sentence added that to protect themselves some nuns had taken birth control pills. *They what?*

Like Don Quixote, article in hand, I went forth to the next class. An opening came with, "Are there any other questions?"

"Father, is it true that birth control is always a sin?" I asked.

"Yes," he answered.

"So there are no instances when it is not sinful?"

"That's correct."

"Then how is it not sinful for nuns in Africa to use birth control?"

Shuffling feet froze, papers quieted, eyes ricocheted between Father Farraher and me.

With Johnny Carson timing he responded, "Birth control is a sin of the married."

And with that, class ended.

The fact that I struggled with moral theology didn't surprise me. It reminded me of my high school combat with Father Menard over the Church and Galileo. The struggle now took place on a deeper theological level. I came away feeling like Camus' Sisyphus, eternally pushing a huge rock up the hill only to see it roll back down where the process would begin again.

Father Meyer

Father Meyer arrived at Alma College at the same time as our class. He came with a freshly minted doctorate in theology from the *Universita Gregoriana*, the flagship of orthodox Catholic theology moored in Rome and referred to as "the Greg." But Father Meyer was not a typical Catholic theologian. His journey toward the doctorate had begun at Alma College. Before encamping in Rome, he had studied at the University of Strasbourg, a citadel of Lutheran scholarship, and Gottingen

University, known not only for its free-thinking theology, but also for giants in physics like Max Born, Max Planck, and J. Robert Oppenheimer.

We knew his expertise concentrated on the "historical Jesus," the arena where history and theology focus on the authenticity of Jesus' existence and what Matthew, Mark, Luke, and John had written about him. Sitting in class, I observed this late-thirties, reddish-haired professor adjusting his glasses and his gaze, which tilted slightly upward as if looking for his next thought on the ceiling at the back of the room. At times he seemed lost in a trance as he reeled off references to Rudolf Bultmann and Ernst Kasemann, Protestant scholars famous for their pursuit of the historical Jesus. He never referred to non-Catholic experts as "Protestant" or "Lutheran" or "Baptist"; they were simply some of the "best in the field." I suspect Pope John XXIII's ecumenical reign had thawed the glacial edges of Catholic scholarship, and allowed Father Meyer to study with Jesus experts from other denominations.

In the spring of 1966 Father Meyer convinced the faculty to welcome a guest speaker who would address the entire student body. The guest was an *uber* scholar of Jesus, Ernst Kasemann. Father Meyer had forewarned us that his English was limited. Most of us managed the heavy seas of Kasemann's German accent when he read from prepared notes, but when his enthusiasm carried him into a sidebar comment, he was forced to turn to Father Meyer to solve an English word-search problem. There then ensued a back-and-forth exchange in German that sounded like the classic Abbott and Costello comic routine, "Who's on first?" Eventually, the right word emerged to make the point at hand, now lost to the audience during their exchange. What was not lost between these two scholars was their fraternal warmth and shared pursuit of the historical Jesus.

Father Meyer's history lectures on Jesus segued into his courses on the "Founding of the Church" and the "Nature and Mission of the Church." In these courses, he steered into the shoals of my faith. Given my growing skepticism about the Church's doctrine on sin, its moral position on birth control, and its mixed message on personal conscience, I reacted to any comment that touched the raw nerves of my inflamed doubt.

Stunned by what I thought I had heard Father Meyer say in a mid-March class, I sought him out privately. Whether it was purposeful or just the fate for a new faculty member, Father Meyer was assigned living quarters, actually a small study with an alcove for his bed, in the bowels of Alma College. My visit felt like a walk on the stairs in an Escher drawing; I descended a steep staircase near the kitchen, where another set of stairs descended further, both of which followed the sloping hill, which a mile later ended at Highway 17. The descent to his room brought the smell of cigarette smoke drifting up through a hallway made, like most of Alma College, of compressed paper over cedar framing. My imagination ignited a brief fear of what could happen if Father Meyer became careless with one of his lighted Camels.

He welcomed me with a warm smile and an invitation to sit in the chair he quickly cleared of books and periodicals.

"Father, I've been thinking about your last lecture and I'm here to make sure I correctly understand what you said," I began.

"What part of the lecture?"

"It was the part where you were discussing the relationship between personal conscience and the dictates of the Church. Did I hear you correctly that if a woman believed the Church was the supreme authority on a matter of morals and chose to violate one, like practicing birth control, she would be committing a mortal sin?"

"Yes, that's accurate."

"And I also thought I heard you say that if the Church were to erroneously declare a particular act immoral, it could not be the true Church of God because it would have become an 'agent of death,' condemning people to eternal damnation based on false doctrine."

"Yes, that's true."

At that moment, I was shaken. I was sure that Father Meyer knew where I was going with this line of questioning. His manner was eerily nonplussed. He didn't ask me why I asked the questions. I sensed we were Jesuit co-conspirators in a modern-day Guy Fawkes plot. Only years later did I learn that he left the Order in 1969 to begin teaching theology in a non-Catholic institution. However, I knew immediately I couldn't quarantine my doubts. I needed to sift through them with someone I could trust.

FATHER DAILEY

Not long after my chat with Father Meyer, I jotted down a list of people I might talk to about my mushrooming doubts. The unwritten rule of not disclosing to peers troubling thoughts removed most of those I lived with. The available confessor for theologians was a pleasant retired Australian Jesuit known for ending his talks with the encouraging refrain, "Keep your peckers up." No one had the heart to tell him that "pecker" was not, for American males, our first synonym for "nose." I didn't think he'd be a good fit for what ailed me.

There was a charismatic professor of dogmatic theology whom many found very helpful. In brief conversations I'd had with him, I couldn't follow his abstract profundity and quickly dropped him from the list.

Father Dailey, a moral theologian known for his ability to listen and to understand even poorly expressed questions, kept coming to mind. I had never talked to him one-on-one. I'd heard from those a year ahead of me that his teaching style was open and never authoritarian. He was not known as a maverick or renegade. Perhaps it was his not fitting the stereotype of a moral theologian, at least not one who rigidly parsed sin and downplayed the Inquisition's treatment of Galileo, that drew me in his direction. I had noticed his easily awakened smile and steady measured walk that exuded balance. Intuitively I felt talking with him might be helpful. There was irony in choosing a professor of moral theology, the subject that triggered much of my personal turmoil, to help me examine the inner workings of that turmoil.

I knocked on Father Dailey's door. My knock was met with a simple, "Come in." As I stepped in, I caught sight of him sitting at his desk in a flowered Hawaiian sport shirt. Books askew on the shelves behind him framed his salt-and-pepper hair, thick glasses, and easy half-smile.

"I'd like to talk with you for a few minutes if you have the time," I said.

He motioned me to the chair in front of his desk as he eased back from the writing I'd interrupted.

"What brings you in?" he asked.

"I'm not really sure. I guess I need help sorting out a lot of thoughts and feelings that make me feel detached and out of synch."

"Tell me more about the tangle of thoughts and feelings."

"I feel I'm caught in middle between the demands of church teachings and the demands of my conscience. To say the least, that's painful."

"Is that what seems to be giving you the 'out-of-synch' feeling?"

"Yes, I feel painted into a hypocritical corner in learning how to absolve people for sins I don't believe are sins, like birth control. Sometimes I feel angry being put in that position. How can I personally reject an act as sinful, and then act as if it were sinful in absolving a penitent who confesses it as a sin?"

"You're finding a disconnect between what you believe and what you feel you are called to do."

"Yes, that's a big part of it."

And that began the first of many sessions spanning the next several months.

MEDITATION AND FAITH

For over nine years, meditation had begun the day, before Mass and breakfast. It remained a daily staple aimed at feeding my spiritual life. During the Novitiate and Juniorate, 5:30 a.m. meditation brought me to my knees on the hard wooden kneeler that was part of our sparse furniture. Sleep stalked me as my shoulders sagged forward and the weight of my torso automatically shifted to forearms. The quick drop of my chin snapped my neck and roused my attention and drove back sleep as I recovered enough to refocus on the business of prayer. I revisited my personal lexicon of sleep-evading tactics: biting my tongue; standing and holding a meditation prompt—New Testament, crucifix, picture of Christ—or opening the window to cool air.

Even after years of practice, meditation challenged me. It's true, Father Elliott, my novice master, had instructed me on the basics of "discursive meditation," which shares a lot with a good speech. It's divided into three parts: preparation—typically, selecting a scripture or a passage from a spiritual writer; then meditation proper—imagining a scene, reflecting on the event or passage, and talking to Jesus or God; and then a petition or resolve. The rhythm of Ignatian meditation was intellectual, a probing for inspiration or insight that would end in some form of action. Ignatius wanted us Jesuits to be "contemplatives in

action" as opposed to pure contemplatives who remained se-
questered in a monastery. But after Father Elliott's brief introduction to meditation, I had been on my own.

Many times during meditation, I felt I was looking through
binoculars straining to see God on a planet in a galaxy well beyond our Milky Way. And because I was supposed to know how
to meditate, or was too embarrassed to admit I didn't know
what to do, I drifted. It struck me as odd that such an important
activity, the engine of Ignatian spirituality, never came with a
better set of directions or an open forum where we could trade
tips on what works and what doesn't.

Meditating in Oregon, Washington, and California certainly brought unique places to meditate—kneeling in a chapel,
pacing in a hallway, or, at Alma College, walking outside in the
travelogue beauty close to the Santa Cruz Mountains.

Just after daybreak at Alma, weather permitting, I would
follow the path around the lake with its geyser fountain. It was
here I came several times in the spring of 1966 to meditate on
thoughts gleaned from *Encounters with Silence,* a slim volume
authored by eminent Jesuit theologian Karl Rahner. I hoped
it might be a grappling hook to catch hold of the rock of faith
and stop my slide into disbelief.

Rahner writes of God as "so eternally hidden in the abysses
of Your Infinity that it leaves behind in creation no sign that
we could make out by ourselves...." followed shortly by, "For us,
only the finite and tangible is real and near enough to touch:
can You be real and near to me, when I must confess You as
Infinite?" A little later, "What poor creature You have made me,
O God! All I know about You and about myself is that You are
the eternal mystery of my life. Lord, what a frightful puzzle man
is! He belongs to You, and You are the Incomprehensible...."

Rahner re-tolled a theme heard in Augustine and Thomas
Aquinas—God is a mystery. I thought if God is a mystery and

a mystery is beyond human grasp, why do theologians unceasingly try to parse Him? Only faith builds a bridge to belief in God. And my faith was in short supply.

Was I really meditating or just being distracted by random thoughts? It was hard to tell the difference, especially during the annual eight-day retreat, when the number of meditations was doubled or tripled. My first retreat in theology again had brought me face to face with the first sentence of Ignatius's thirteenth rule for thinking with the Church: "If we wish to be sure that we are right in all things, we should always be ready to accept this principle: I will believe that the white that I see is black, if the hierarchical Church so defines it." The fervor was gone that had led me past that rule during the long retreat in the Novitiate and subsequent retreats. I now felt only a lobotomy would lead me to accept it. Was there room for my questioning?

Hope

The spring semester of 1966 came to an end with final oral examinations. In many of the classes that form the core of Jesuit education, the examinations are conducted in Latin. An exception was *Moral Theology I-B* because it consisted of the Jesuit student confessor hearing the Confession of a penitent role-played by one of three examining professors. Each examiner rendered a score ranging from one to ten, with a six equivalent to a C. A semester of poring over texts, periodicals, and lectures, together with a maelstrom of moral dilemmas ranging from birth control to war, backlit the final examination. Minor issues fighting for their place on the head of a theologian's pin, already crowded with angels, were not worth discussing.

My disillusionment with moral theology, theology in general, and my future role as priest advocate for Catholicism weighed me down. I worried about what questions I'd be asked and whether my answers would disclose my loosening belief in Church teaching. I tried not to fret. I opted for God's will; His will be done. Besides, my examiners may simply want to know whether I can credibly do the job of a confessor absolving people of their sins and comforting them in their human frailty.

Easing down into the simple, unpadded chair behind a bare, four-foot wide wooden table, I faced the three faculty examiners who were there to put me through my moral theology paces. If it were a close role-play of a real Confession, I'd rotate my chair a quarter turn to the left leaving the examiners on my right. Then I'd be in the same position a priest would have sitting in a confessional, with a listening ear tilted toward a veiled wooden grate and the penitent's subdued voice. However, with the fresh air of openness let in by grandfatherly Pope John XXIII, face-to-face confessions had become common. Hence, it made sense for this day and for this examination to look directly at my priest examiners.

After fifteen minutes of warm-up questions testing basic common sense, Father O'Hanlon stepped up the challenge.

"Father Tracy," he said, "Your penitent is Sister Agnes, who has asked to go to Confession." He paused and continued as Sister Agnes: "Bless me, Father, for I have sinned. My last Confession was two weeks ago. Since that time I've read erotic literature and had impure thoughts."

"What are you referring to when you say 'impure thoughts'?" I asked.

"I'm talking about becoming sexually aroused when reading a novel."

"Why were you reading the novel?"

"I'm taking a graduate course in English literature and part of the assigned reading is *Lady Chatterley's Lover* by D.H. Lawrence."

"So you were reading the book as part of an assignment toward your degree and became aroused while reading it?"

"Yes."

"Were you reading the novel for sexual gratification?"

"Definitely not, it was assigned reading."

"Sister, do you think celibate religious people should not have sexual feelings?"

"No, of course not. But I feel I crossed a line. I should have stopped sooner. I should have exerted more control."

"I don't think God expects us to have such control over our bodily responses."

"But he does expect us to be careful and to avoid occasions of sin."

"And Sister, from what you said, you were reading the novel as part of a class assignment and not for sexual gratification."

"Yes, that's true."

"What degree are you pursuing and how long will it take to complete?"

"I'm finishing my second semester of what will be a five-semester program for my master's degree."

"It sounds like it will take you a lot longer if you have to interrupt yourself every time you encounter stimulating material. Sister, I believe you encountered the sexual side of your humanity that God blessed you with. Short of acting out your sexuality, I believe a compassionate God sees your reactions as normal reactions not to be inflated into sins. Can you accept this?"

There was a lengthy pause. "Well, yes."

"And for your penance I want you to read the next two chapters of *Lady Chatterley's Lover.*"

I felt calm and relieved following the exam, as if I'd finished a complete basketball game in thirty minutes. I left the room and walked down the covered walkways attuned to the beauty of the golf course lawn, the smell of flowers I couldn't name, and a breeze between the classroom and dormitory wings.

Within twenty-four hours, grades emerged in threes, one number grade from each examiner, such as 8-9-8 or, God forbid, 6-6-6. I received a 10-10-10. Surprised, pleased, and pensive, I wondered whether I might fit into this life after all.

CHAPTER 11

Summer School 1966

UCLA

I didn't know what I was in for. Attending UCLA was my first college experience outside a Catholic citadel of learning. Not until I had arrived on campus did I feel the quantum leap it really was. UCLA's campus was several times larger than Seattle University, where I'd spent two summer schools. All my university learning had blossomed in the hothouses of Catholicism. At Gonzaga and Seattle U, lay students showed reflexive respect for our cassocks and Roman collars. I certainly didn't expect and didn't receive the same treatment at UCLA. I was just another student.

The closest reminders of anything religious on campus were red-brick Italian Renaissance buildings—Royce Hall, with its twin church-like towers, and the Powell library, with a sixty-foot dome and octagonal tower. Both struck me as expatriated and remodeled churches from Milan or Verona. They stood as centerpieces spawning several modern, but always red-brick, offspring.

Each morning, the campus hummed to life as I and hundreds of other students arrowed our way to class. Most of the time at UCLA I wore black slacks and a short-sleeved black shirt fitted with a Roman collar. At first, I imagined I stuck out among the mid-sixties tie-dyed T-shirts, shorts, and Southern

California get-ups. I soon realized I moved along unnoticed in the tides flowing in and out of classes.

My upper division class in tests and measurements was an independent study requiring only meetings with the professor. My course in learning theory required daily class lectures with weekly tests. I settled into absorbing the theories of rat-running psychologists like Hull, Guthrie, and Skinner. During the second week of class, a curly headed fellow in the first row broke into the professor's monotone lecture with, "When are we going to learn about human learning? All we hear about is rats, rats, rats!" The professor, a well-published visiting professor, slowly turned his tall, thin frame toward the student, like a tank turret rotating to zero in on a target. In a flat, firm voice he replied, "The difference between rats and men is only quantitative." Then he resumed his lecture. I realized psychology too preached dogmatic beliefs, not ones I was about to challenge at this time. I had more than enough dogmatism to deal with in theology.

The class in learning theory and meetings with the professor overseeing my independent study left plenty of time in the early afternoon to study and explore the campus. I developed a routine of buying a sandwich and searching out a bench or an outdoor table where I could spend thirty minutes eating and people-watching. These noon-time lunches brought back memories of when I was eight and recovering from my second bout of rheumatic fever. Back then, while lying on my back on the grass, I'd catch sight of a high-up airplane and wonder about the passengers and where they were going. Now I was scanning the faces and strides of students on the move and wondering why they were there and where they were going in life.

During a mid-summer stretch of particularly hot weather, I decided for one day to substitute a short-sleeved sport shirt for the clerical black shirt and Roman collar. After eating my sandwich and discarding the wrapper in a bin twenty feet from where I'd been sitting, I returned to the table to find a coed sitting opposite with her back to me. She turned and said she didn't know someone had been sitting there, although my books were in plain sight. Because the table and benches could easily accommodate six people, I said, "There's plenty of room."

"What classes are you taking," she asked.

"Psychology," I said.

We chatted briefly and benignly about the demands of class. She was taking art history. After ten minutes, I said I had to be going and left to study in the library. I wondered whether she noticed the guy she had been talking to probably was the only male on campus wearing full-length black slacks on a sweltering day. I wondered whether she would have spoken to me had I been sporting my Roman collar. I wondered whether brief exchanges like we had sometimes blossomed and endured. I never saw her again, and my random search for places to eat lunch never took me back to that table again.

CHANCE MEETING

Mike, an ex-Jesuit, dropped by Loyola University several times to visit former brothers in black like me. After he had left the Jesuits, Mike settled in LA, where he worked for Allstate Insurance and lived near Redondo Beach close to Loyola. Besides fraternizing with us, he came to see his second cousin, Sister Maria, a Providence nun who was taking courses at Loyola. In late June, I found him chatting with Jesuits, his cousin, and another nun from her Order (in social setting nuns typically moved in pairs). The hum of conversation matched the buzzing bees close by, thriving in the rose gardens on campus.

I perked up when Sister Maria mentioned a Sister Rebecca was the on-campus superior for the Providence nuns. I asked whether this Sister Rebecca had ever taught at St. Catherine's in Seattle. I found she had. She had been my favorite grade school teacher, probably because she liked me. Her concern for my fragile health seemed as strong as Mom's. I wanted to see her again.

Twenty years had etched a few crow's feet close to Sister Rebecca's twinkling eyes. Still youthful in her mid-forties, her smile and upbeat manner matched the young nun who'd taught me when I was seven. When she asked what brought me to Loyola, I described classes at UCLA, especially the testing course that had begun to worry me. In her motherly way, she dug to the root of my present worry—recruiting thirty respondents for a psychological questionnaire I was developing.

She immediately said, "I can help with that."

As a superior on campus, she held the power to direct the nuns under the wings of her authority. My hunch was she would slip a soft glove on the hand of authority and add a story about one of her grade-school students, now a Jesuit, who needed their assistance.

Later in the week, Sister Rebecca shepherded a flock of twenty-eight Providence nuns, including Sister Maria, into a white-walled classroom filled with the small desk-seat combinations, which offered neither comfort nor a decent writing surface. I had arrived early, attired for the occasion in collar and cassock, to set up my handouts and to rehearse the patter I'd use to sell a dull task. Stepping forward to the elevated dais, I caught my foot on the inside of my cassock and catapulted forward. My outstretched arm prevented a full head-plant. I heard no laughter and saw no faces about to break out into a what-a-klutz smile. The tough part of my request was breaking the news that I needed the group to return in a week to complete another parallel questionnaire. Again, I saw no rolling eyes and heard no sighs. The aura of charity and obedience permeating religious life was working in my favor.

The fervor of the priests, nuns, and seminarians living on campus didn't rule out "worldly" moments. Thanks to the generosity of a Loyola University benefactor, first-run Hollywood films came on Friday afternoons for the enjoyment of the seminarians, nuns, and priests on campus. In mid-July *The Flight of the Phoenix,* starring Jimmy Stewart, drew over a hundred religious of various orders to an improvised outdoor theater. A fellow theologian and I found seats amidst the swirling crowd of black dotted with color. We Jesuits, sometimes seen as avant-garde mavericks, added Technicolor to the sea of black-and-white religious habits with the florid sport shirts we often wore on campus.

As I sat down, I recognized Sister Maria sitting close by with another Providence nun. I made a point of thanking her for participating in the coerced test-taking. Waiting for the show to start, I made small talk by asking the nuns what classes they were taking. The conversation tiptoed into sharing what religious books we were reading. It turned out that Sister Maria and I were both reading *The Secular City* by Harvey Cox, a non-Catholic Harvard theologian who advanced the revolutionary thesis (revolutionary for Catholics) that the Church was not an institution but a group of action-oriented people. Our conversation gave way to Jimmy Stewart jerry-rigging the carcass of a crashed DC-3 into a flying machine that escapes the thirsty sands of North Africa.

In addition to movies, music also brought male and female religious together. Besides the singing at Sunday Mass, there were sing-alongs. I was dragged to one organized by a recently ordained Jesuit with a Frank Sinatra voice. The rationale I'd heard for singing was it would be a relaxing break for the religious students on campus. I knew the Jesuit next to me was an accomplished tenor, while I was well aware of my off-key warble. Peers since the Novitiate had joked about my voice punishing any future congregation where I might be sent to sing High Mass. I sat down in the outer ring of two circles of nuns and seminarians in the amphitheater. I regretted giving into the pressure to come along. I didn't know the words to any popular songs and felt out of place. I couldn't bring myself to join in the singing, although I do remember the thrumming beat of Peter, Paul, and Mary's "If I Had a Hammer" as I slipped away.

I wanted to be by myself to filter sense out of the feeling of being out of place. The detachment ran deeper than sing-along discomfort. *Was it just this evening? Did it come from the whiplash of moving each day from religious Loyola to secular UCLA and back again? Was it knowing that at the end of summer I'd return to the study of theology?* I recall slowly climbing the dormitory stairs to my room, walking down the hall to an alcove that housed a bin of soft drinks, and fishing through the slushy ice for my nightly Seven-Up. My chilled hand reminded me that this soda was a summer luxury that would end with my return to Alma. Often, it was the most enjoyable event of the day.

A Model

The following Saturday, I was intent upon reading another chapter in Kimble's text on learning theory when I came across Mike chatting with his cousin and her companion nun on the path that crisscrossed between the dorms. After pausing for a polite hello, I stayed a bit longer, probably a resistance to the dry reading beckoning me to my room. Just before I left, the topic of where we would be living in the fall came up. I said I'd return to theology studies at Alma College and the companion nun mentioned the school where she would be teaching.

However, Sister Maria said, "I'm not free to say where I will be in the fall." The response struck me as a bit odd, but not enough to provoke a follow-up question.

In the late afternoon the next day, a Jesuit in my dorm relayed the message that Sister Maria had asked to speak with me. My first thought was her request might be tied to our interrupted talk on *The Secular City*. Seeing her on the grounds after supper, I suggested we meet, after I returned from UCLA on Monday, in the Loyola Jesuit residence where the full-time Jesuit faculty resided year-round. I chose to have the meeting in one of the clear glass parlors in full view of anyone entering or leaving the residence. It was not usual for male and female religious to meet one-on-one.

Wanting to be above reproach, I arrived on Monday not in my casual sport shirt but in formal Roman collar and cassock. Sister Maria, in her austere black habit, sat waiting outside the fishbowl parlor. She was petite and a foot shorter than me. A few freckles lurked beside large, clunky glasses that obviously didn't cost her Order much. The tightly fitted garniture surrounding her face hid every strand of hair, but not her high cheekbones. After ushering her into the glass-and-wood-paneled parlor, I had to wait just a moment before she said, "I want to explain my evasive answer on Saturday."

"The one about not being able to say where you'd be living next year?"

"Yes, I couldn't answer because I'm leaving the Order and am not supposed to tell anyone."

My mind flashed to the unwritten rule I knew well. I surmised the Providence nuns, an Order heavily influenced by the Jesuits, must have the same code of silence regarding those who leave the religious life.

I thought of the Novitiate, where a departed brother's absence, his name no longer on the list of chore assignments or his chair empty in Latin class, was never discussed. I had face-tiously wondered whether we would have been told had he been struck by lightning or a truck. The same silence had shrouded exits in the Juniorate and philosophy studies. But now, in theology, there was the scintilla of notification: on the bulletin board a single straight pin skewered a three-by-five card announcing, "Mr. X left the Order yesterday." While I could understand the reason for not speculating about the reasons why people left religious life or not having a tearful wake in their honor, I still thought the taboo about those who left the Order was carried too far.

"You felt it wouldn't be proper to mention you're leaving, especially with the Sister who was with you?"

"That's right. Even now I feel a bit awkward telling you, but still I'd like to talk to someone about what I'm facing."

I felt a flash of anger at the cruelty of forbidding a person to discuss what she's facing after several years in religious life.

"What you're facing?"

"Since I let my parents know I'd be coming home, my dad has written and encouraged me to stay. He's really disappointed. He's a strict Catholic, raised in a family of ten kids. He believes he'll get a higher place in heaven if his daughter is a nun."

"Guilty?"

"I don't feel guilty about leaving the Order. I'm sorry he's upset, but not guilty. He's an old-fashioned rigid Catholic."

"What else are you facing?"

"Lots of pressure. I know I'm a good teacher but leaving this late in the summer will make it hard to get a teaching job this fall."

I was sitting in an odd spot. As with students at Bellarmine discussing *Civil Disobedience*, I didn't need to tell her what to think or how to make sense of what she was going through. I relied on Carl Rogers and Father Dailey.

An hour went by quickly. We both knew we needed to return to our dorms and prepare for separate meals.

"Being able to talk to someone is such a relief," she said.

"Would you like to chat again?"

She hesitated, then said, "I don't talk much."

"Well, I don't think silence will be a problem."

We agreed to meet outdoors in the afternoon later that week rather than in the formal parlor. I felt comfortable moving our meetings from the faculty residence to a walk on the paths of campus, open to the scrutiny of passing cars, priests reading their breviaries, and students walking to their dorms.

Reflecting on our chat, I guessed her choosing to talk to me flowed partly from my living under the same mantle of religious life and partly from my involvement in psychology. I guessed she saw me as a safe person to talk over what she was thinking and feeling. Based on what I had learned in my counseling courses, I resolved at that moment not to share any of my own doubts and struggles with theology, religion, or the religious life. Personal disclosure could easily muddy the waters of what she wanted to talk about. Carl Rogers' non-directive method, which had helped me while teaching high school, fit our talks.

I didn't count the number of times we met to walk up and down the shaded path that stretched from the dormitories down to the university entrance and paralleled the ten-foot-wide swath of rose bushes that separated the entrance and exit lanes to Loyola. In the late afternoon tall trees provided shade from the western sun tanning the swimmers at Hermosa Beach a mile away. The breeze cresting the hill perched above Howard Hughes' private airfield perfumed the walkway with the fragrance of roses. The breeze also brought the thump-thump-thump from a bunker below the hill where Hughes was rumored to be developing a super machine gun for the Vietnam War.

The ironic mixture of beauty and war provided the backdrop for the slow stroll and the steady way Sister Maria moved from concerns about her future to reflections about the religious life she was shedding. She voiced her shock at being told early in training that her questioning intellect was the devil's workshop, a warning she came to reject over time. I was careful to limit my response to, "It sounds like over time you couldn't accept that." And that reflection triggered her talking of the hobbled role of women in the Church. Her words, like Robert Frost's "how way leads on to way" in *The Road Not Taken*, retraced the steps leading her to leave religious life.

In mid-August, classes were ending and I prepared to return to theology and Sister Maria prepared to become Jean Talbott once again. At the end of our last walk, I gave her Viktor Frankl's *Man's Search for Meaning* and asked her to let me know how she was doing after she returned home to Seattle and got settled. She promised to send back the book together with a status report.

On the drive way back to Alma, I reflected on my meetings with Sister Maria. I was pleased that I had not mixed my doubts with what she needed. Admiration for her courage and honesty revved my eagerness to get back to sessions with Father Dailey

CHAPTER 12

Second Year Theology

After returning to Alma from summer school, I learned of a chance to get away with five friends, classmates who were organizing a trip to Yosemite National Park. I eagerly signed on. We scrounged together camping gear, an aging Chevy Suburban, and a bare-bones allowance to give us almost a week to explore a place I'd only seen on postcards.

The gray-granite face of Half Dome rising four thousand feet from the valley floor made me wonder whether some prehistoric giant had split a mountain in half. Leaning back to look up, I teetered on the edge of vertigo. The breeze was a whisper carrying the smell of pine. The clean air brightened the surrounding colors—green, brown, and yellow—making them as vivid as a new plaid shirt. Soaking up the beauty of Tuolumne Meadows and Porcupine Flat, cooking hamburgers over a fire pit, melting marshmallows and Hersheys into gooey s'mores, and sleeping in a chilly tent—all this done together in fraternal give-and-take—rekindled the feeling found only in family. Yosemite succeeded in keeping at bay, for a few days, doubts that were closing in. I sensed a storm not far off, like those I knew came when a cold front met a warm one and rumbled in the mountains.

Getting Started Again

The eight-day retreat, our yearly refresher course in the Spiritual Exercises, immediately followed my return from Yosemite. After the Novitiate's first thirty-day version, each annual retreat had grown more familiar, like spring training for professional baseball players. This tenth repetition re-plowed the field of personal sinfulness and re-planted the seeds of redemption through Christ. This time I broke away from the retreat-giver's lockstep presentation to focus on parts of the *Spiritual Exercises* demanding my attention. Again I carefully reread the rules. I viewed my meetings with Father Dailey as in step with the *Rules for the Discernment of Spirits*. His attentive acceptance and comments like, "That sounds like a frustration you need to address," had kept me focused and confident. I was not distracted by a fear of an evil spirit misguiding me. However, I still resisted the thinking-with-the-Church rule, "If we wish to be sure that we are right in all things, we should always be ready to accept this principle: I will believe that the white that I see is black, if the hierarchical Church so defines it." That rule strikes at the heart of inquiry.

Sitting across from Father Dailey was comforting. His relaxed posture and steady gaze invited me to start where I wanted. I shared the sense of detachment I felt during the summer. I talked of the strength I'd seen in Sister Maria, how she had forged a difficult decision on her own.

"I've been trying to figure out why moral theology grates on me. It strikes me as contamination of conscience. It's fine to call out the sinfulness of hatred, murder, and infidelity, but in any way to equate eating meat on Friday and birth control to them seems ridiculous."

"Where does that put you?"

"I find myself in a dull, stalled place."

"A stalled place?"

"I feel like I can't go forward."

"What do you need to do to get out of the stalled place?

"I need to sort, to keep what's essential and let go of the rest."

Shortly after that it was time to stop.

I delayed dealing with the storm the retreat had triggered by looking into the future. At some point, graduate school will demand passing one, maybe two, foreign language examinations. I decided to buttress my shaky French, not by studying grammar, but by reading. Digging in the library unearthed *L'Etranger* (*The Stranger*) by Camus whose *Myth of Sisyphus* had piqued my interest at Bellarmine. Armed with a French dictionary, I attacked the Frenchman's novel, which was really philosophy cloaked in a story. A few hours struggling with the French put me in full retreat. I generously estimated my comprehension of the French text at less than fifty percent. I switched to an English translation.

The emotionally withered principal character, Meursault, pulled me into his alienation just as the absurdity of *The Myth of Sisyphus* had drawn me in two years before. His jail house exchanges with the chaplain, who vainly tried to save his murder-stained soul, outshined the self-righteous pity of the priest. Meursault felt happy approaching his execution with the thought that "I opened myself to the gentle indifference of the world."

Meursault's talk with the priest brought back James Joyce's Stephen Daedalus, who had haunted me in philosophy—how Daedalus turned his back on what the Jesuit had offered. My present reaction differed from the one five years earlier. I didn't feel disoriented. I sat adrift in a boat a failed knot had freed from the dock.

AN EXCHANGE OF IDEAS

I don't recall the particulars of how it came about—"it" being a symposium on the role of religion in contemporary society. It began on Friday afternoon in September 1966 and extended through late Sunday, just prior to the beginning of fall term. The setting was classic California in the early autumn: seventy-five degrees, an ambivalent breeze over the 50-foot-wide tailored lawn separating the classroom wing from the dormitory wing, birds signaling their hidden presence inside the thick bushes rimming the grass rectangle that ran toward the upper buildings.

Sport shirts and casual slacks were the dress du jour. Invited attendees included California college faculty as well as theologians from nearby Protestant seminaries. They totaled five, with two added from our faculty, and filled the seven chairs arced at the front of our largest classroom. We student theologians, over one hundred strong, sat waiting for the exchange to unfold. The symposium was promoted as an "exchange of ideas." Reflecting the ecumenism of Pope John, who had called the recent Vatican Council and tried to let fresh air into a stuffy Church, this exchange had gathered scholars with divergent views. The Rector, Father Farraher, welcomed the outsiders with the hope that we would all be richer for the openness and respect we'd share over the next few days.

Dr. Adler of California State College at Los Angeles followed the rector's generic opening with, "I'm here to honestly exchange views about the role of religion in society today. But I have two questions regarding my invitation to participate. The background to the questions is the fact that I'm a non-believer, an atheist. So here's the first question: 'Was I invited just to be a stimulus for you to formulate better arguments against atheists like me?' I'm here to listen sincerely and openly and I'm prepared to change my view if your religious perspective is persuasive. My second question is: 'Are you open enough to change your mind?'"

Wow, what a show-stopper! I had no way of knowing whether anyone else had the same thought or whether any of my fellow theologians were having trouble with the positions we were being trained to take into the world.

The initial discussion among the faculty participants focused on whether religious teachings like the Ten Commandments formed the basis of ethics. The exchange was respectful and low-key. While a few questions from the student audience were accepted, the format prescribed smaller breakout groups to continue the topic. Because there weren't enough non-Jesuits to go around, I sat with a small group of my peers.

Daryl, one year ahead of me, spoke first in my group.

"Christ is the bedrock of my ethics. In fact, without my belief in Jesus Christ I couldn't be ethical. I could imagine myself easily becoming a psychopath exploiting other people and taking advantage of them every chance I could."

"Do you really believe psychopathy would be your fate if you didn't believe in Jesus?" I asked.

"Yes, I do."

Turning to the four others I asked, "How many of you believe you'd become heartless, selfish human beings devoid of an ethical sense if you didn't believe in Christ?"

No response.

Not knowing how to deal with the deafening silence, I asked, "Do you think a secular humanist or a non-Christian can lead an ethical life?"

"I don't think they'd be able to consistently maintain an ethical life without Christ," Daryl answered.

"So do you think Jews, Muslims, and atheists are less able to live an ethical life because they don't believe in Jesus Christ?"

"I firmly believe that they would be better equipped to live an ethical life if they espoused Jesus in a formal way."

"Do you have serious doubts about Dr. Adler's ability to live an ethical life, given his avowed atheism?"

"That's not for me to judge," replied Daryl.

I was irritated with Daryl's evasive response, which failed to mask his self-righteous judgment. Pushing the issue seemed pointless.

The rock-and-roll of these small group discussions sprinkled the mid-afternoons, while a formal group presentation kicked off each morning and set the theme of the day. Discussions spilled over to meal times and the after-dinner beer-drinking. I came away with mixed feelings—upbeat at the thought of the healthy openness of many of our guests, discouraged by what seemed to me a pervasive Church disease, hardening of doctrinal categories.

The hope of fitting into Jesuit life, which the positive grades on my spring Confession exam had triggered, dimmed as I realized that the gauntlet of openness Dr. Adler had thrown down the first day remained on the ground.

FAITH IN THE FACE OF DOUBT

With the end of the symposium, I turned to an unfinished talk I had agreed to give at the Cal Berkeley Newman Club, a religious center for Catholics attending public colleges. Four of us in my class had agreed to give a series of eight talks, ironically entitled, "Faith in the Face of Doubt." I was to lead off with "Faith and Growth: A Psychology of Faith."

One part of the talk drew on my recent reading of parts of Teilhard de Chardin's *Phenomenon of Man*. I was less intrigued with this controversial Jesuit's blend of evolution and philosophy than I was with how the Church had treated him. While scientists had honored de Chardin for his contributions as a paleontologist, the Church had forbidden him to write or teach philosophy. In addition, the Church had denied him more than once the authorization (*imprimatur*) to publish the *Phenomenon of Man*. Even after his death in 1955, the Holy Office (successor to the Inquisition) had urged Church authorities to protect the minds of the young against the dangers of his writing. I couldn't stop the sinking feeling. This Jesuit's recent journey ended like those of Galileo and Erasmus—bending their knees to the dictates of the Church.

Three weeks later, a blustery wind tugged at my black raincoat as I found my way from the car to the Newman Center. I struggled to stay confident in my talk, organized with what I hoped was a minimum of psychological jargon. I worried about the question-and-answer session that was to follow. I was keenly aware of the obligation to walk the tightrope between giving honest answers and excessively candid ones. Even as I thought about the honest-candid distinction, I recalled the unflattering adjective "jesuitical," a person who excels in equivocation. I'd just do my best.

"Father Tracy, you said there was a balance between personal autonomy and the authority of the Church. But then you went on to say that there are times when we may have to choose. Would you say more about that?"

"In the spirit of honesty, I need to clarify my status as a seminarian and not yet a 'Father.' Regarding your question, I would cite Thomas Aquinas's position on the primacy of a well-informed conscience over the authority of the Church, even in the case of heretics. Hopefully, those instances are rare. The challenge is to be careful and prudent, with an eye wary of emotion overcoming reason."

That response to a tough question, among several that were easier to address, helped me escape the question-and-answer exchange without, I hoped, damaging the faith of students who had come out on a windy night.

The drive back from Berkeley gave me time to reflect on the tight feeling that I'd felt before the talk. *What was I uptight about?* The tenseness consisted of one part nervous expectation in speaking to an unknown audience for the first time; the other nine parts boiled down to fear of being dishonest. I was sure the audience would be made up of smart people, individuals who could easily sniff out glib reasoning. As I drove along, reverie accompanied the headlights that pushed the dark away. I imagined myself locked in a photographer's dark room opening canisters filled with the undeveloped film of my Catholic life. I saw film deep in the solution where chemicals made latent images visible. There was Father Menard and me with my Galileo notes, Father Dempsey holding my David Copperfield report, Father Meyer telling me when a church would become an instrument of death. There I also found film from the future—myself teaching psychology at Seattle University, instructing engaged couples on Catholic marriage. One question kept surfacing: "Could I be honest and a priest?"

Closure

It was a pleasantly warm Los Gatos afternoon when I left my room on the cooler east side of the building for a late afternoon session with Father Dailey. I saw Joe, a recently ordained fourth-year theologian, coming down the hall toward me. His glistening wet hair, the towel slung over his shoulder, and flip-flops clapping on the floor made it obvious he was returning from the showers. The custom of not talking in hallways, a holdover from Novitiate days, had loosened enough over the years to make his smile and nod a "Hi." Like many of the newly ordained theologians who blossomed with ordination, his face sparkled. I couldn't help feeling envious, especially when I was heading to Father Dailey's room for another chat about items that put me at odds with the priesthood.

After settling into the now familiar leather cushioned chair and bouncing theological odds-and-ends off Father Dailey for forty minutes, I stopped talking and sat silent. I knew this priest-therapist would patiently wait for me to come back from wherever I had gone.

"I think I'm beginning to piece together the thousand-piece puzzle of me," I began.

"Do you feel you have enough pieces to create a picture?" he asked.

"I'm not sure, but enough to give it a try."

"Where would you start?"

"I know I've moaned and whined about the Church's position on birth control and the conflict between personal conscience and Church authority and a lot of other things, but when I step back to get perspective, the only way I can fit together the specific issues is "the Church.""

"The Church?"

"Up to this point, the Church has always been the bedrock in my life that supports my connection with God. Now it's become a rock I've run aground on."

"And that leaves you?"

"Well, I'd say I'm stuck on an object that definitely has no give, especially to one guy in a rowboat."

Father Dailey casually reached over and closed tight the venetian blind on his window next to the outside walkway, a reflexive move he had made during many of our sessions. Today, it struck me as a fitting in a meeting room filled with conspirators. The air in the room stood still. He repeated, "And that leaves you?"

"I think I have to face the fact that the Church and I are at an impasse. And the Church is certainly not going to change its dogma or moral positions for me. Intellectually it would be easy to say, 'The Church and I have to part company,' but that's easier said than done."

"And that leaves you?"

"It leaves me with an issue I need to sort out before I come back again."

"I'll be here," he said. His facial expression, like a faceted precious stone, seemed to hold simultaneously seriousness, warmth, empathy, and always acceptance.

I nodded, rose, and left knowing I needed to put more pieces of the puzzle together.

Over the next week, I retreated to the chapel mid-afternoons, when there was rarely anyone else there and where it was always a few degrees cooler than my room. There I struggled to get over the barrier that made it hard to think of leaving the Order.

With my fellow Jesuits I had shared a vision Ignatius outlined and Pope Julius III approved in 1550 with: "Whoever desires to serve as a soldier of God beneath the banner of the cross in our Society...is a member of a Society founded chiefly for this purpose: to strive especially for the defense and propagation of the faith and for the progress of souls in Christian life and doctrine."

My ten years in the Order always, implicitly at least, had marched to the beat of that goal. Now, in the study of theology, I found the faith hard to defend, almost impossible to propagate, and key parts of the doctrine unbelievable. And Ignatius requiring me to believe the white I see is black had become a reach too far.

It was now clear to me that waves of doubt had been washing away the Catholic foundation on which my life in the Order had rested. What was hardest for me to imagine was giving up the company of dedicated, intelligent men I'd lived with, studied with, prayed with, vacationed with, and drank beer with. I felt connected to "The Company of Jesus," the name of the Order long before it became known as "Jesuits." And the word "Company," which came from the Latin *cum pane* ("with bread"), captured an essential part of community life—eating together. As familiar as the air I breathed, the life I'd been living was filled with a sustaining sense of companionship, even though that companionship cordoned off the expression of feelings.

During the week following my meeting with Father Dailey, I continued to seek out the path around the lake where I'd grown accustomed to walking during morning meditation. Now, I walked there after evening recreation when tall evergreens cast their shadows far out on the lake and the ducks were still bobbing for food in the shallow water close to the edge. The evening's just-finished bridge game took its place with the shared study groups, basketball games, and retreats that stretched back over ten years. The thought of needing to let go of that bond made me wonder whether it's the emotion one experiences riding to a brother's funeral.

The next Monday, I sat down in Father's Dailey's room and said, "I've come back to pick up where we left off."

"And where in particular do you want to pick up?"

"I think you said something like, 'And where does that leave you?' which was between the rock of a Church I can't in good conscience defend or propagate and the hard place of giving up the camaraderie of the Order."

"A very real rock and hard place."

"It would be easier in many ways to ride the wave of comradeship through theology and ordination than to leave the Order now. But I know that would not be honest and just delaying the inevitable."

"The inevitable?"

"I see the 'inevitable' emerging like an iceberg in the fog that I'm either going to collide with or miss only by changing course. My best estimate is, I'm facing a choice point where I'd eventually have to leave the Order for lack of belief in its mission or stay on to become a shell of a Jesuit like the dean of studies James Joyce described in *The Portrait*. No matter how much I value and feel the companionship of the Order, it can't be the reason for my staying on."

"It sounds like you've reached a decision."

"I have."

"And do you see any way I can be helpful?"

"I'd appreciate your support and help in going through all the steps involved in leaving."

Leaning forward with his arms on the desk, he joined his hands like doors gently closing and said, "I'll be happy to do that."

And that brief session led to working with Father Dailey to craft a letter, in Latin of course, to Pedro Arrupe, the General in Rome. The letter summarized my current questions and conclusions regarding the religious life, my lack of fit for the priesthood, and my difficulties with the Church.

The General's reply letter in English, dated November 9, 1966, included, "...you should ask for your release now and find your place in another state of life while you are still young...." And with that confirmation I took the final step of setting up my exit with the Provincial in Portland.

Ironically, the next day I received a letter from Jean Talbott telling me that she was returning by separate mail *Man's Search for Meaning*, the book I had given her at Loyola. She wrote that she liked it very much and went on to briefly describe her landing a job teaching first grade and adjusting to life outside the convent. The next day I replied with a short note saying that I was leaving the Order and hoped my landing back in Seattle went as well as hers. I made a mental note that she was a person who'd likely understand my struggle and decision to leave the Jesuits.

CHAPTER 13

Exit

W ith my decision to leave the Order made, I began map-
ping my exit. The most obvious step was to coordinate
exit paperwork through the Provincial's office in Portland.
The documents would formally release me from my vows, as
well as sever my association with the Order. D-Day (Departure-
from-the-Order Day) was set for December 6.

NIHIL OBSTAT

After lunch in late November, I found a neatly folded note stuck
on my door. The message directed me to see Father Wright, a
new addition to the faculty. I had not yet taken a class from him
or even talked to him. Since my Novitiate days in the Order,
I had heard about this Oregon Jesuit who'd become a theological titan at the prestigious Gregorian University in Rome.
I'd seen him walking to class with a stride so smooth that he
looked as if he were gliding on ice skates.

Why was I being summoned to see him?

I found his room and the chair where he beckoned me to
sit. He sat forward at his desk with a single closed manila folder
in front of him. There wasn't a hint of gray hair in the few dark
strands neatly combed over the top of his balding head. His

wire-rimmed, thick glasses shrunk his far-sighted eyes, which peered at me above a faint smile.

"Thank you for coming," he began. "I've been asked to review your paper you presented on the Berkeley campus. I do have a few questions I'd like to ask."

Opening the folder in front of him, he said, "I noticed that you make a comparison between Teilhard de Chardin and Martin Luther."

Immediately, I sensed the reason behind our meeting. I had mentioned to a few people a week before that I was fine with the plan to submit all the Berkeley talks for publication. I did know any publication related to the Catholic faith or morals had to pass through a censor and receive a *nihil obstat* (nothing objectionable stands in the way of it being published). The Church's canon law requires such clearance before a publication is forwarded to a bishop for an *imprimatur* (let it be printed).

These hurdles are what this meeting is all about.

"Do you think the comparison you made is an apt one?"

"I do think that both men were being asked to repudiate what they were saying. I understand that Father de Chardin signed a withdrawal of specific teachings and exiled himself in China."

"Have you considered any ways of reworking your talk for publication?"

"Hopefully, readers will see my primary point—both de Chardin and Luther were censored by the Church; one found a way to remain in the Church, the other did not."

Father Wright nodded his head in a noncommittal way. He rephrased the same question a few more times before bringing our ten-minute exchange to a close.

I don't think Father Wright suspected that his reluctant agreement that nothing stands in the way of my article being published ran parallel to my knowing that nothing stood in the way of my leaving the Order.

I came away wondering how I would feel at this moment had I chosen to remain in the Society. However, this authoritarian nudge toward conformity stirred no reflexive anger; it felt ironic in the light of my choice.

CHANGING CLOTHES

Another step in the exit process was to get some non-clerical clothing. I drove the winding state highway south to a men's store in San Jose, a store owned by a graduate of Gonzaga. The staff likely knew the drill for outfitting Jesuits, soon to be ex-Jesuits, easily known by the purchase-order we carried. I had been given permission to buy a suit, a shirt, a tie, and a pair of shoes. The salesman was about my age. His light-brown suit, blue shirt, coordinated tie, and wingtip loafers with tassels testified to his outfitting expertise. I wondered whether the hidden hand that guided this exit process had chosen this young man to assist me, just as an older salesman at a mortuary might work best with gray-haired customers shopping for a relative's coffin. Within thirty minutes, I exited the store with a dark brown suit, white shirt, two ties, and brown wingtip shoes.

GOOD-BYES

While there wasn't any training in how to leave the Order, I knew well the unwritten protocol that surrounded my decision and its action steps, clandestine as a CIA operation. In spite of the unwritten injunction against talking to peers about leaving the Order, I decided to tell a few of my closest friends.

I noticed George Dahlquist's cassock hanging from a hook on the back of his door as I closed it. He rotated toward me in his swivel chair where he sat in a frayed T-shirt and black trousers. The goose-necked lamp on his desk bounced light from the lacquered surface of his desk and backlit his querying eyes. Over the years, we had moved side-by-side through the Novitiate to the Juniorate, where together we departed early for summer-school chemistry at Gonzaga. The end of philosophy brought the two of us to regency at Bellarmine. Now, he'd caught up with me in theology. Over the years, I'd seen his reddish blonde hair retreat from thin, to strands, and now to shiny baldness. He shot me his vintage half-smile, which some viewed as dullness, but which I had come to know was just the surface of the depth he possessed, a depth masked by the slow pace of his conversation.

"George, I've come to tell you I'm leaving the Order."

Rolling his chair away from the desk and turning fully toward me, he asked, "Why?"

"Without going through a blow-by-blow account of how I reached the decision, the reason is I've come to realize I'm not a good fit for the Order."

He paused, looked at his hands and then at me with eyes that had filmed over. He stood and shook my hand. No more words were needed. Neither of us possessed the vocabulary for what we felt. I turned and left.

I found the other good-byes similarly quiet and brief. I didn't elaborate the regret I felt in separating from the best and only fraternity I had known, from men I had grown with over ten years. I wondered whether they would have acted any differently had I said I was joining a team of astronauts leaving for a planet deep in our Milky Way.

FLYING OUT

Flying north to Portland, I mulled over my journey in the Order. I'd adhered to the vows of poverty, chastity, and obedience. I'd never really felt a burden from poverty, because food, shelter, and education had never been wanting; chastity was never a burning St. Augustine issue, because I was naïve and had only experienced adolescent sexual experimentation; obedience was the tough one I'd never mastered. It had caught me in a swing dance between blind acceptance and chronic questioning.

I slipped into my window seat on the Boeing 707 flight out of San Francisco. Images of what the formal resignation would be like flitted though my head. Webbed in thought, I took little notice of the man who took the seat next to me. Coat off, white shirt and tie, banter with the stewardess, then his question broke in.

"And what do you do?" he asked.

I scrambled for a way to avoid a story he was probably not interested in and I definitely didn't want to tell. "I'm not free to talk about that," I replied.

My answer unhorsed his inquiry and gave me the opening to counter with, "What do *you* do?"

He launched non-stop into a 30-minute monologue about his sales career, one that didn't stick in my mind. It did push the subject away from me into his life. He eventually wound down and I settled into looking out the window at the shelf of clouds below us. I hadn't thought to bring a book. I swung between studying the bland blue-red-gray pattern of United Airlines fabric and faking a catnap.

"Would you care for a cocktail?" the stewardess asked.

"No, thanks" I answered.

"I bet you didn't know you had the CIA on board did you?" chirped the salesman.

She didn't answer.

The cocktail he ordered restarted his monologue, which droned on until our descent into Portland.

During the landing approach, he asked, "Do you need a ride anywhere? I have a car."

Stifling a reflexive "No, thanks," I knew no one was picking me up. A ride from him would be faster than a taxi.

"Yes, I'd appreciate that," I said.

Riding down SE Powell Boulevard in Portland, I pulled the Provincial's address from my coat pocket and planned my next move.

"If you could drop me off on SE 45th Avenue, that'll be great," I said.

I'd calculated that would put me just three blocks from my destination.

As he rolled to a stop, I thanked him for his generosity in giving me a lift. I stood on the corner following his face in the side-view mirror looking back at me until he turned onto Franklin and out of sight.

SIGNING OUT

Anonymity intact, I marched the final few blocks to the gray stone building housing the administrative center for the Oregon Jesuits. The ambiance of the cloudy Portland day and the gray granite mansion seemed right out of Count Dracula's Transylvania.

I was ushered into a polished dark mahogany foyer that led to a broad, sweeping staircase to the second floor. An exit story from the Novitiate flooded into my mind. The gist of the story was that upon signing papers to leave the Order, the now ex-Jesuit fell to his knees, having been struck by the foolishness of resigning, only to be told his decision couldn't be undone. This image of wailing and regret was interrupted by, "Hello, I'm Father Meany, assistant to the Provincial. Please follow me."

The Provincial's Residence, Portland, Oregon

The late-thirties Jesuit led me up the stairs to an office where we were joined by Brother Calouri, whom I'd known at Sheridan. The priest pointed to a chair close to a spacious desk topped only with two one-page documents. After I sat down, I scanned the closest page, which was in Latin and pre-signed by the Provincial. It contained a declaration that I was leaving the Society legitimately and was free of my vows. The second document contained a single paragraph in English with a carbon copy beneath. It read that I had received "the sum of two hundred dollars ($200) in full payment of all claims against the said Society and against all houses, Colleges, Universities, Churches, and persons in the same Society and Province." After I signed this settlement for my ten years, three months, and twenty days in the Order, the two Jesuits added their signatures as witnesses. I didn't feel tremors of remorse or urges to reverse my decision. Neither did I experience euphoria. A surreal calm mingled with gratitude for the years of Jesuit companionship, the wide-ranging education, and Father Dailey's counseling.

On my cab ride to the Portland Airport, I caught a glimpse of the Columbia River, which triggered a memory of salmon-fishing in Puget Sound with Dad when I was eleven. We had been caught in a storm off Whidbey Island, two miles from the boathouse in Mukilteo, where Dad had rented the open sixteen-foot "kicker" boat. The six-horsepower outboard motor struggled to keep the heavy wooden craft moving. Strong winds had deepened several waves, which hit us sideways and left five to six inches of water at the aft end, where Dad sat steering with the outboard's single handle. After making slow progress eastward against the strengthening wind, Dad turned northwest toward the Whidbey beach and eyed a spot with no logs or large rocks. Just before we landed he gunned the motor and drove the bow a few feet up on the beach to secure us. We scrambled out and Dad tied the bow line to a log higher on the beach. At first, the motor and aft end bobbed in the surf. But soon the high wind and waves pivoted the boat sideways and began pouring more water into it. Dad stood tall and erect, facing the howling wind. His face took on a determined look as he stared off toward where we'd started. I waited with my eyes locked on him.

"We're going back out and across to the boathouse," he said firmly. He shot me a glance filled with a message I immediately decoded. *Landing here didn't work out. We're reversing course and going to make it back to where we started.*

Dad calmly gave me clear instructions, "Tighten your life vest and sit in the bow. Because the wind will keep the bow high and will block my view, you'll have to help me by pointing where the big waves are coming from."

The salt water spray stung my eyes and blurred my vision. The wind and the slapping waves made yelling back to Dad useless. Like a policeman directing traffic, I pointed in the direction of the most threatening waves so Dad could tiller the boat into them and avoid sliding sideways into a trough that might swamp us. We worked together for what seemed like hours, but likely was less than one, and safely made it across to the boathouse. I felt the same relief now in the cab taking me to the airport for the final flight to Seattle.

CHAPTER 14

Life Unfolding

A fter a week back in Seattle and out of the cassock and Roman collar, I felt natural in a suit and tie. I wore the new outfit to the bank, where I opened an account, and to my first job interview. After Christmas, I found the letter from Jean Talbott inside the book she had returned to me, and used the return address to find her parents' telephone number. I gave her a call.

By mid-January, Seattle Central Community College hired me to work as a vocational counselor with high school drop-outs. In early April, I received a September acceptance to graduate school in psychology at the University of Connecticut. By that time, Jean and I had been seeing each other regularly, and I was confident that we were a match. She was initially concerned about our relationship rebounding too quickly from the religious life to married life. But together we dissolved her hesitation, and were married in August. We honeymooned across Canada, and then dropped into New England. Only in retrospect do those nine months blur like a speed train. At the time, I found them pleasantly paced.

GRADUATE SCHOOL AND ETHICS
"Without Christ I would have become a psychopath," and its accompanying innuendo, stuck with me after I left the Jesuits.

Like an annoying pebble in the shoe, that statement and the tone of the fellow theologian who said it still irked me. The subtext asserted that the atheist professor who attended our ecumenical gathering at Alma College was incapable of living an ethical life without the help of Christ. I'm sure my aversion to the comment pushed my master's thesis and doctoral dissertation to investigate moral judgment. In those graduate school projects, I pursued what I had begun in philosophy eight years before—finding a basis for ethics independent of religion.

MOVING AHEAD

Our first son arrived not long before I earned my degree. Soon afterwards, we moved to Bryn Mawr College in Pennsylvania. There I taught while Jean earned her graduate degree in social work. Then we returned "home" to the Northwest, where our second son was born and our careers accelerated.

In this jet stream, Jean and I grew closer as we developed our careers and coordinated our schedules in raising our sons. The speed of living came close to overtaking the headlights beamed into the future. Only intermittently did I step back to reflect how fortunate I had been in meeting Jean, raising a family together, and finding satisfaction as a psychologist.

THE CHALLENGE OF DEATH

In 2001, breast cancer briefly disturbed the flow of my living. I treated it as a lump on the road and quarantined any implications for the future. Eight years later, at a dinner hosted by a friend of Jean's, the friend's husband made a passing comment about the benefits he had gained from a Buddhist retreat. I noted that he was science-oriented and worked in high-end computing. I asked a few questions, and found out where the retreat took place.

Over the next several days, recurring thoughts cycled through my mind. *I've passed more than midlife; I'm on the down-hill side of living.* I missed the comfort of Catholicism with its guarantee of eternal life after following Church teachings and living an adequately good life. Like the cat who swats the pros-trate mouse to see if there's life left, I had begun poking at religions and literature. Yama of the Hindus, Egyptian Anubis, Thanatos of the Greeks, Santa Muerte of Mexico—all hint at what's in store for us.

THE BUDDHIST RETREAT

The ten days of silence, each filled with ten hours of medita-tion, certainly introduced me to "impermanence." My concen-tration frequently flitted off to the discomfort that comes with maintaining a position for an hour. Calm interludes sometimes bubbled up after the swirl of distractions and physical pain gave way to concentration. I found mortality and tongue-in-cheek humor in the teacher saying, "No itch or pain lasts forever."

I was surprised to learn that Buddha was an atheist who dis-missed the notion of a god, one who might assist me in develop-ing a spiritual life, or send me to heaven or hell. That revelation made me move Buddhism from a religion to a philosophy, be-cause I'd never heard of a religion that didn't believe in a god. I found it interesting that believers were welcomed to learn Vipassana meditation as long as they suspended their religious practices during the ten days of the retreat. In the course of my first retreat, the Buddhist teacher gave me an article prais-ing Vipassana authored by Father O'Hanlon, the professor who had role-played the nun during my moral theology exam at

Alma. His kudos for Buddhism fit with the high grade he gave the unorthodox penance I had given the penitent nun.

After ten days of silence, we were free to chat with one another.

"Why are you here?" asked the lightly bearded, early-twenties fellow whom I had never met before. He stared at me and waited for an answer.

"I've come in search of a peaceful attitude for facing death," I replied.

My young questioner broke eye contact, uttered "Oh," and walked away.

I'm not sure whether my answer shocked or merely puzzled the young man. My answer made me aware that I'd come full circle since age six, when I had begun my Catholic trek as a sickly first-grader. Back then, I studied the Baltimore Catechism, laden with what I had been told were the right answers. Now Vipassana had helped me sample moments of *upekkha* (equanimity), awareness that senses the moment free of emotional lows or highs. Buddha was right; all living things come into being, endure for a while, and then pass away. I would be no exception. And that is OK.

CHAPTER 15

Epilogue

L eaving the Jesuits marked the point at which my faith in the Church sat close to empty. I could not accept the Vatican's position on moral issues like birth control and divorce. I reviewed with fresh eyes specific church dogmas, which had faded like color photographs too long in sunlight. Within the first year, my belief in the Catholic Church as the mediator between me and God stopped.

WHERE I STAND

With the Church removed, I was alone with God. I'm using the word "God" in the broad sense, which includes Jesus Christ. I no longer believed that a loving God exists, one who is interested in every human being and with whom believers can develop a personal relationship. The notion of an eternal Being seemed no more or less credible than energy eternally cycling back and forth with matter.

For a time, I considered "Pascal's wager." Blaise Pascal, French mathematician and philosopher of the seventeenth century, reasoned that I could choose either to believe or not to believe that God exists. If He exists, I win either infinite happiness or infinite pain (heaven or hell). If He doesn't exist, I lose a finite amount of happiness, like the amount of time spent going to church and observing rituals. But I view Pascal as playing the odds on an outcome, while I am more interested in being honest about my belief. I'm betting that if God exists, He or She will judge me on the basis of how well or how poorly I have lived my life. Whatever comes with dying, I want to meet it honestly and head-on. I don't want to be sucked down from behind while frantically paddling away from the whirlpool of my mortality.

In one way I am an atheist, because the Greek word αθεος means "without God." I live my life without asking what God expects of me each day, without asking God to grant me favors or to protect me from evil. However, I do not rule out the possibility of God's existence. Hence, for those who like to categorize, "agnostic" fits me better. As an agnostic, I respect those who believe in God, like my wife. I have no reason to rant against those who believe in God, or to call them stupid, or to bring lawsuits over the use of the word "God" in the Pledge of Allegiance. Still, I will confront theists who attempt to impose their God on me or to restrict my freedom not to believe. Some, I'm sure, believe I am destined for hell.

MYSTERY

My childhood recovery from the first round of rheumatic fever had awakened wonder about "infinity." Wonder became the fertile ground from which questions had grown. I memorized answers in the Baltimore Catechism, which I still can recite today.

Q. Why did God make me?
A. God made me to know Him, to love Him, and to serve Him in this world, and to be happy with Him forever in the next.

Q. Who is God?
A. God is the Creator of heaven and earth, and of all things.
Q. What is God?
A. God is a spirit infinitely perfect.

Such questions lead to the unfathomable waters of mystery, a topic the Catechism also addressed.

Q. What is a mystery?
A mystery is a truth which we cannot fully understand.

My father made the same point about limitation in his own way: "You can't put ten pounds of flour in a five-pound bag."

I've concluded that two kinds of mystery exist: what's unknown and what's unknowable. The first encompasses all those things we humans don't know at the moment but are likely to discover eventually, things like the cures for many cancers and whether rational beings exist on distant planets. The second kind of mystery drops us into the black hole of our inherent limitations.

When I think of limits, I think of Chum, the most intelligent dog I've ever owned. She was a blond Labrador mix whose coat felt like velvet. She reflected my moods with her drooping ears or wagging tail. She would chase down, bring back, and drop at my feet the golf ball I'd pitched deep into the thick woods tangled with undergrowth behind our home. But I don't believe she possessed the capacity to reflect on her own abilities, or on what it would be like to be a human being. In spite of her remarkable intelligence, she came with canine limits.

For me, Chum's limits parallel the human limits regarding impenetrable mysteries. I believe there are questions that exceed our capacity to answer, questions like "Why is there something rather than nothing? Can God be understood? Is there existence after this life?" Unlike Chum, however, we humans can reflect on the boundaries of our capacity to know. If we are honest, we must admit at this time that we simply don't have the capacity to answer certain questions. For many, faith bridges the gap between their human limits and unfathomable mystery.

LIVING MY LIFE

Before we were married, Jean asked, "What do you think love is?"

"I don't know," I said. (Certainly not an endearing thing to say.)

Over our nearly fifty years together, I have come to experience love as being as tangible as my breath. For me, love eludes the empirical rigor of science, but that fact makes it no less real. The love Jean and I share comforts and enriches me. Of that, I'm certain.

My life is not over yet. I plan to continue following the desire to know, which brings satisfaction as I answer the questions I can and note the mysteries beyond my reach. My daily challenge is to remain "equanimous" as I pursue truth and wisdom.

I have gleaned wonderful advice about living life from Buddha, Socrates, Jesus, Ben Franklin, and a few comedians. I've distilled the following guidelines from examining age-old virtues. They help keep me looking inward and outward.

* Treat others as you want to be treated.
* Help others, even those who can never help you in return.
* Be generous without being taken advantage of.
* Know your personal strengths and weaknesses.

+ Be honest.
+ Keep commitments.
+ Listen openly to those who disagree with you.
+ Be wary of opinions wrapped in too much emotion—
  those you hold and those you hear.
+ Don't take yourself too seriously.

In writing this memoir, I've come to realize how top-heavy I am. My thinking towers over my emotions, and any mystical side is yet to make itself known. I'm doing my best to better balance the first two, and will be pleasantly surprised if the third blips on my radar. And if God reveals himself, I hope his infinite wisdom and love will judge me on how honestly I tried to live.

Influential Works

Here is a partial list of the works of authors mentioned in the memoir together with others that did or are influencing me.

Augustine. (1960). *The Confessions of Saint Augustine.* (J. Ryan, Trans.) New York: Random House.

Baltimore, T.P.C. (1885). *A Catechism of Christian Doctrine.* Chicago: Benziger.

Brooks, D. (2012). *The Social Animal.* New York: Random House.

Camus, A. (1955). *The Myth of Sisyphus and other essays.* (J. O'Brien, Trans.) New York: Vintage Books.

Camus, A. (1989). *The Stranger.* (M. Ward, Trans.) New York: Vintage Books.

Chardin, P. (1959). *The Phenomenon of Man.* (B. Wall, Trans.) New York: Harper Row.

Haidt, J. (2013). *The Righteous Mind.* New York: Vintage Books.

Holt, J. (2012). *Why does the World Exist?* New York: Liveright Publishing.

Holy Bible NSRV. (1989). New York: HarperCollins.

Huizinga, J. (1957). *Erasmus and the Age of Reformation.* (F. Hopman, Trans.) New York: Harper Torchbook.

Joyce, J. (1993). *A Portrait of the Artist as a Young Man.* New York: Penguin Books.

Kaufmann, W. (1961). *Faith of a Heretic.* Garden City, NY: Doubleday & Co.

Lonergan, B. J. (1958). *Insight: A Study of Human Understanding.* London: Longmans, Green and Co.

Loyola, I. (1964). *The Spiritual Exercise of St. Ignatius.* (A. Mottola, Trans.) Garden City: Image Books.

Montaigne, M. (2003). *The Complete Essays.* (M. Screech, Trans.) New York: Penguin Books.

Nagel, T. (2012). *Mind & Cosmos.* New York: Oxford University Press.

Piaget, J. (1965). *The Moral Judgment of the Child.* (M. Gabain, Trans.) New York: Free Press.

Pieper, J. (1952). *Leisure the Basis of Culture.* (A. Dru, Trans.) New York: Pantheon Books.

Rahner, K. (1960). *Encounters with Silence.* (J. Demske, Trans.) Westminster, MD: Newman Press.

Acknowledgments

Jean has traveled beside me for close to a half century, read every word of this memoir, offered wise edits, and given me her love.

My sons, daughters, grandchildren, and extended family encouraged me.

My brother, Ron, added and corrected family memories.

Gary Miranda skillfully edited the entire manuscript and clarified many of my Jesuit memories.

Writers Wendy Call and Carlene Cross offered their professional advice.

Members of my writing group—John Andrew, Marion Kee, Laura Rankin, Amy Scott, Ludmila Shebeko, and Janet C. Thomas—offered many helpful suggestions for more than five years.

Father Peter Ely and Father Frank Case graciously read the manuscript and tweaked my Jesuit memory.

David Kingma, archivist at Gonzaga University, helped me exhume parts of my Jesuit history.

Made in the USA
Charleston, SC
23 March 2016